AI and Machine Learning in Action: Real-World Solutions for Coders

By **Aniket Jain**

Copyright © 2025 by Aniket Jain

All rights reserved. No part of this book may be reproduced, distributed, or transmitted in any form or by any means, including photocopying, recording, or other electronic or mechanical methods, without the prior written permission of the publisher, except in the case of brief quotations embodied in critical reviews and certain other non-commercial uses permitted by copyright law.

For permission requests, please contact the author at aniketjain8441@gmail.com

Disclaimer

The views and opinions expressed in this book are solely those of the author and do not necessarily reflect the official policy or position of any organization, institution, or entity. The information provided in this book is for general informational purposes only and should not be construed as professional advice.

Publisher

Aniket Jain

Table of Contents

1. **Introduction to AI and Machine Learning**
   - What is Artificial Intelligence?
   - Understanding Machine Learning Concepts
   - Why Python is Perfect for AI and ML
   - Setting Up Python for ML Development (Anaconda, Jupyter, etc.)

2. **Getting Started with Python for Machine Learning**
   - Python Basics for AI: Libraries and Tools
   - Introduction to NumPy, Pandas, and Matplotlib
   - Writing Your First Python Script for Data Analysis

3. **Working with Data in Python**
   - Loading Datasets with Pandas
   - Data Cleaning and Preprocessing in Python
   - Feature Engineering with Scikit-Learn
   - Data Visualization with Matplotlib and Seaborn

4. **Supervised Learning in Python**
   - Linear Regression: Building Your First Model in Python
   - Logistic Regression for Classification
   - Decision Trees and Random Forests

- Evaluating Models: Accuracy, Precision, and Recall
- Real-World Example: Predicting House Prices

5. **Unsupervised Learning in Python**
    - Clustering with K-Means in Python
    - Dimensionality Reduction: PCA Implementation
    - Real-World Example: Customer Segmentation Using Python

6. **Deep Learning with Python**
    - Introduction to Neural Networks
    - Building a Neural Network Using TensorFlow and Keras
    - Convolutional Neural Networks (CNNs) for Image Classification
    - Real-World Example: Handwritten Digit Recognition (MNIST Dataset)

7. **Natural Language Processing with Python**
    - Text Preprocessing with NLTK and spaCy
    - Building a Sentiment Analysis Model in Python
    - Real-World Example: Creating a Python-Based Chatbot

8. **Reinforcement Learning in Python**
    - Fundamentals of Reinforcement Learning
    - Implementing Q-Learning in Python

- Real-World Example: Building an AI for a Simple Game

9. **Deploying AI Models with Python**
    - Exporting and Saving Models
    - Building Flask APIs for AI Predictions
    - Deploying AI Models Using Streamlit

10. **Ethics and Challenges in AI Development**
    - Mitigating Bias in AI Models
    - Ensuring Data Privacy in Python Applications
    - Real-World Considerations for Ethical AI

11. **End-to-End AI Projects in Python**
    - Project 1: Predicting Stock Market Trends
    - Project 2: Real-Time Face Recognition with OpenCV
    - Project 3: Sentiment Analysis for Customer Feedback
    - Project 4: Image Classification with CNNs
    - Project 5: Text Summarization with NLP
    - Project 6: Recommendation System for E-Commerce
    - Project 7: Time Series Forecasting for Sales Data
    - Project 8: Object Detection in Images

- Project 9: Fraud Detection in Financial Transactions
- Project 10: Chatbot for Customer Support

12. **Resources for Learning Python-Based AI and ML**
    - Top Python Libraries for AI and ML
    - Recommended Courses and Books, Apps
    - Staying Up-to-Date with AI Trends in Python

1. Introduction to AI and Machine Learning

What is Artificial Intelligence?

Artificial Intelligence (AI) refers to the simulation of human intelligence in machines that are programmed to think, learn, and adapt to new situations. These systems are designed to enable computers to perform tasks that typically require human cognitive abilities, such as understanding natural language, recognizing complex patterns, solving intricate problems, and making informed decisions. AI spans a broad spectrum, from simple algorithms tailored for specific tasks to highly sophisticated systems capable of self-learning and continuous adaptation. This dynamic nature of AI allows it to grow and evolve over time, potentially transforming every aspect of human life.

AI's development has been fueled by a convergence of advanced algorithms, vast computational power, and the availability of massive datasets. Its applications range from enabling self-driving cars to detecting diseases earlier than traditional methods. Additionally, AI continues to redefine industries such as manufacturing, agriculture, and entertainment, offering innovative solutions to longstanding challenges.

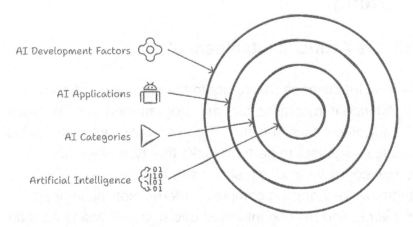

AI and its Ecosystem

The overarching goal of AI is to develop systems that can operate autonomously, exhibit intelligent behavior, and refine their capabilities through the process of learning. Such advancements hold promise for revolutionizing fields such as healthcare, finance, education, and more. For example, in healthcare, AI-powered systems can analyze medical images with incredible accuracy, assist in diagnostics, and predict patient outcomes based on historical data.

AI is commonly classified into two broad categories:

- **Narrow AI**: This type of AI is designed to perform a specific task efficiently. Examples include voice-activated virtual assistants (e.g., Siri, Alexa), recommendation engines used by streaming services, and automated customer support systems. Narrow AI

excels in predefined domains but lacks the ability to generalize across different tasks.
- **General AI**: This represents the pinnacle of AI research and development. General AI aims to replicate human intelligence in its entirety, allowing machines to perform any intellectual task that a human can accomplish. While still a theoretical concept, it is a focus of ongoing research and exploration in the AI community. The vision for General AI involves creating machines that not only think like humans but also reason, understand context, and solve problems creatively.

Comparing AI's Present and Future Capabilities

Understanding Machine Learning Concepts

Machine Learning (ML) is a subset of Artificial Intelligence (AI) that focuses on the creation of algorithms enabling computers to learn and improve their performance using data, without the need for explicit programming. This paradigm shift allows systems to adapt to new data inputs and optimize their operations based on insights derived from patterns and inferences, bypassing the limitations of traditional programming methods. ML's versatility makes it particularly well-suited for addressing complex and dynamic problems that require continuous learning and adjustment.

Key concepts in ML include:

- **Supervised Learning**: This approach involves training algorithms on labeled datasets where each input is paired with a corresponding output. The algorithm learns the mapping between inputs and outputs to make accurate predictions on new, unseen data. For example, identifying whether an email is spam or not based on historical data.
- **Unsupervised Learning**: In this method, the algorithm works with unlabeled data, seeking to uncover hidden patterns, structures, or groupings. Applications include clustering customers based on purchasing behavior or reducing data dimensionality for visualization. Unsupervised learning is particularly valuable for exploratory data analysis.
- **Reinforcement Learning**: This technique trains algorithms through a reward-and-penalty system, much like human trial-and-error learning. The goal is to maximize rewards while performing tasks, such as teaching a robot to navigate a maze or optimizing strategies in games. Reinforcement learning has gained prominence in fields like robotics and autonomous systems.

Machine Learning applications span various domains, including spam email detection, image and speech recognition, predictive analytics for forecasting trends, and personalized recommendation systems. The transformative potential of ML continues to grow as advancements in algorithms and computational power expand its capabilities. As industries increasingly adopt ML technologies, the demand for skilled practitioners capable of designing and implementing these solutions continues to rise.

Why Python is Perfect for AI and ML

Python has emerged as the go-to language for AI and ML development due to its simplicity, flexibility, and the vast ecosystem of powerful libraries it offers. This combination makes Python uniquely positioned as a favorite for both beginners and seasoned developers seeking to create sophisticated AI models and systems. Its versatility allows developers to prototype quickly, experiment extensively, and deploy efficiently, making it an indispensable tool in the AI and ML toolkit.

Some advantages of using Python:

- **Readability and Ease of Use**: Python's clean and intuitive syntax simplifies complex coding tasks, enabling developers to focus entirely on implementing algorithms and conducting experiments without getting bogged down by the language's technicalities. This simplicity accelerates learning and productivity. Beginners can quickly grasp Python's structure, while

experts can leverage its advanced features for intricate projects.
- **Comprehensive Libraries**: The Python ecosystem includes specialized libraries like TensorFlow, PyTorch, Scikit-learn, Pandas, and NumPy, which significantly reduce the effort required to handle mathematical computations, data manipulation, and model building. These libraries often come with detailed documentation and active community support, making them accessible to a wide audience.
- **Community Support**: Python boasts one of the largest and most active developer communities in the world. This vast network continuously enriches Python's resources through tutorials, open-source contributions, and forums, ensuring that help and innovations are always accessible. Developers can find answers to nearly any question, from basic usage to advanced troubleshooting.
- **Cross-Platform Compatibility**: Python's ability to run seamlessly across various operating systems ensures that developers can work flexibly and deploy applications to diverse environments without compatibility concerns. This adaptability makes Python an attractive choice for teams working in heterogeneous environments.

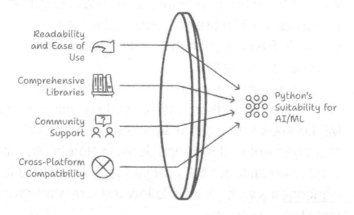

Overall, Python's design and ecosystem have made it a cornerstone of AI and ML development, empowering coders to turn ambitious ideas into reality with unmatched efficiency and creativity. The growing adoption of Python in educational institutions and industries underscores its pivotal role in shaping the future of technology.

Setting Up Python for ML Development (Anaconda, Jupyter, etc.)

Getting started with Python for Machine Learning (ML) requires a well-organized setup that simplifies coding and experimentation. A robust development environment ensures efficiency, minimizes errors, and allows for seamless integration of various tools and libraries.

Here's a comprehensive guide:

1. **Installing Python**: Begin by downloading Python from the official website. Opt for the latest stable version to leverage advanced features and improved performance. Ensure you add Python to your system's PATH during installation to facilitate command-line usage.
2. **Installing Anaconda**: Anaconda is a popular distribution for Python and R, packed with essential ML libraries and tools. It simplifies dependency management and includes Jupyter Notebook, making it indispensable for ML practitioners. Download it from Anaconda's website and follow the straightforward installation process.
3. **Setting Up Jupyter Notebook**: Jupyter Notebook is a powerful tool for creating and sharing documents that include live code, equations, visualizations, and narrative text. Launch it through Anaconda Navigator or from the command line with jupyter notebook. Familiarize yourself with its features, like cell-based execution and inline visualizations, which make prototyping and debugging intuitive.
4. **Installing Essential Libraries**: Python's strength in ML stems from its vast array of specialized libraries. Use pip or conda to install:
    - TensorFlow for deep learning tasks.
    - Scikit-learn for classic ML algorithms.
    - Pandas and NumPy for data manipulation and numerical computation.
    - Matplotlib and Seaborn for data visualization.
5. **Creating Virtual Environments**: Virtual environments isolate project dependencies, ensuring

compatibility and avoiding conflicts. Use conda create or virtualenv to set up isolated environments for each project.
6. **Testing the Setup**: Run a simple script to confirm everything is correctly installed:

    ```
    import tensorflow as tf
    print("TensorFlow version:", tf.__version__)
    ```

    If the script executes successfully, your environment is ready.

7. **Exploring IDE Options**: While Jupyter is excellent for experimentation, Integrated Development Environments (IDEs) like PyCharm or Visual Studio Code can enhance productivity for larger projects. They offer features like debugging, version control, and intelligent code completion.

By setting up a development environment meticulously, you lay the foundation for efficient and effective ML workflows. This structured approach ensures a smooth transition from learning to implementing complex models and deploying them in real-world scenarios.

2. Getting Started with Python for Machine Learning

Python Basics for AI: Libraries and Tools

Python has become the cornerstone of Artificial Intelligence (AI) and Machine Learning (ML) due to its simplicity, flexibility, and extensive ecosystem of libraries. Its universal appeal lies in its ability to cater to diverse skill levels, allowing both beginners and seasoned programmers to innovate with ease. Python's intuitive syntax eliminates steep learning curves, enabling developers to focus on solving complex problems rather than grappling with language intricacies. From prototyping ideas to deploying large-scale systems, Python is the preferred language for AI and ML professionals worldwide.

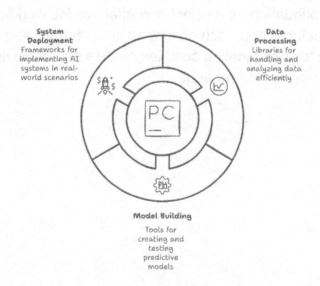

Python's Role in AI and ML

System Deployment
Frameworks for implementing AI systems in real-world scenarios

Data Processing
Libraries for handling and analyzing data efficiently

Model Building
Tools for creating and testing predictive models

The success of AI and ML projects hinges on leveraging Python's ecosystem effectively. This ecosystem is enriched by a multitude of libraries and frameworks that empower developers to process data, build models, and deploy intelligent systems seamlessly. Each library is tailored to specific needs, whether it's numerical computation, data visualization, or deep learning.

Key Python libraries for AI and ML:

1. **NumPy**: NumPy is a foundational library that underpins numerical computing in Python. It facilitates operations on large, multidimensional arrays and matrices, making it indispensable for machine learning algorithms. Beyond basic operations, NumPy excels in advanced tasks like linear algebra, random number generation, and Fourier transformations. Its optimized performance stems from leveraging highly efficient underlying C and Fortran libraries.
2. **Pandas**: Pandas revolutionizes data manipulation and analysis by introducing the DataFrame structure. It simplifies handling structured datasets, enabling developers to clean, transform, and explore data effortlessly. With capabilities like grouping, merging, and filtering, Pandas accelerates data preparation—a critical step before model training. Its compatibility with other Python libraries like NumPy and Matplotlib ensures seamless integration into machine learning workflows.
3. **Matplotlib and Seaborn**: Effective data visualization is key to understanding and communicating insights. Matplotlib provides a versatile environment for

creating plots ranging from simple line charts to complex multi-dimensional visualizations. Seaborn enhances Matplotlib by offering a high-level interface for statistical graphics, making it easier to generate visually appealing plots that highlight data patterns and trends. Together, these libraries are indispensable for exploratory data analysis.
4. **Scikit-learn**: Scikit-learn simplifies traditional machine learning tasks, offering a robust suite of tools for classification, regression, clustering, and dimensionality reduction. Its user-friendly API ensures rapid experimentation, while its preprocessing utilities and evaluation metrics streamline the model-building process. Whether it's a simple logistic regression or a sophisticated ensemble method, Scikit-learn has tools to support diverse needs.
5. **TensorFlow and PyTorch**: These cutting-edge frameworks dominate the deep learning landscape. TensorFlow, backed by Google, is renowned for its scalability and production-ready capabilities. PyTorch, developed by Facebook, is lauded for its dynamic computation graph, making it ideal for research and experimentation. Both frameworks include GPU acceleration, enabling developers to train complex neural networks efficiently on large datasets.
6. **Jupyter Notebook**: Jupyter Notebook transforms the coding experience by blending code execution, visualization, and documentation into an interactive environment. Its cell-based interface allows developers to experiment incrementally, visualize outputs inline, and annotate workflows effectively.

This makes it a favorite among researchers and educators for prototyping and sharing machine learning insights.

By mastering these libraries and tools, developers can harness Python's full potential to solve real-world challenges. From automating mundane tasks to pushing the boundaries of AI innovation, Python continues to redefine what's possible in the fields of AI and ML.

Introduction to NumPy, Pandas, and Matplotlib

These three libraries are the backbone of data analysis in Python. Mastering them ensures you can manipulate, process, and visualize data efficiently—a critical skill for Machine Learning (ML). They provide the tools to handle complex datasets, prepare data for analysis, and communicate results effectively through visualizations.

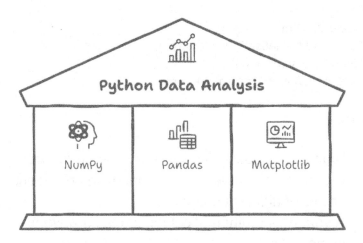

1. NumPy

NumPy forms the foundation of numerical computing in Python. It provides high-performance tools for working with large, multidimensional arrays and matrices. NumPy significantly outperforms Python's native lists in terms of speed and efficiency, especially when dealing with large datasets. Its extensive library of mathematical functions allows developers to perform computations such as linear algebra, Fourier transforms, and statistical operations with minimal code. NumPy is widely used as the backbone of other Python libraries like Pandas, Matplotlib, and Scikit-learn, making it an essential skill for data scientists and ML practitioners.

Example:

```
import numpy as np
array = np.array([10, 20, 30, 40])
print("Array:", array)
print("Mean:", np.mean(array))
print("Standard Deviation:", np.std(array))
print("Sum:", np.sum(array))
print("Squared Values:", np.square(array))
```

Features:

- High-speed operations on arrays and matrices.
- Broadcasting capabilities for handling operations on arrays of different shapes.
- A variety of mathematical functions for advanced computations.

2. Pandas

Pandas simplifies data manipulation and preprocessing by introducing data structures like Series and DataFrames, which make it easy to work with structured datasets. It supports reading and writing data from multiple file formats, including CSV, Excel, SQL, and JSON, making it versatile for real-world data handling. With Pandas, you can clean data, handle missing values, filter datasets, and perform grouping and aggregation, which are all essential steps in preparing data for ML models. Pandas' integration with NumPy and Matplotlib makes it an indispensable part of any Python data analysis workflow.

Example:

```
import pandas as pd
data = {"Name": ["Alice", "Bob", "Charlie"], "Score": [85, 90, 95], "Age": [24, 27, 22]}
df = pd.DataFrame(data)
print("Data Summary:\n", df.describe())
print("Filtered Data (Score > 88):\n", df[df['Score'] > 88])
df['Score'] += 5  # Adding bonus points
print("Updated Scores:\n", df)
```

Features:

- Data wrangling with filtering, grouping, and merging datasets.
- Handling missing values and cleaning data.
- Supports time-series data manipulation for complex datasets.

3. Matplotlib

Matplotlib is a versatile library for creating static, animated, and interactive visualizations. It provides a high degree of control over plot elements, allowing developers to customize their visualizations extensively. From simple line plots to complex multi-layered graphs, Matplotlib serves as a powerful tool for exploratory data analysis. Its tight integration with Pandas and NumPy ensures seamless workflows, enabling quick visualization of data trends, patterns, and relationships.

Example:

```
import matplotlib.pyplot as plt
x = [1, 2, 3, 4, 5]
y = [10, 20, 25, 30, 35]
plt.figure(figsize=(8, 5))  # Adjusting the plot size
plt.plot(x, y, marker='o', linestyle='--', color='blue')
plt.title("Data Trends", fontsize=14)
plt.xlabel("X-axis", fontsize=12)
plt.ylabel("Y-axis", fontsize=12)
plt.grid(True, linestyle='--', alpha=0.7)
plt.show()
```

Features:

- Wide variety of plots, including line, bar, scatter, and histogram.
- Customizable visualizations with titles, labels, and annotations.
- Integration with Pandas and NumPy for efficient visualization workflows.

By mastering NumPy, Pandas, and Matplotlib, you can build a strong foundation in data analysis, which is essential for any ML or data science project. These libraries allow you to process data efficiently, uncover patterns, and present results effectively.

Writing Your First Python Script for Data Analysis

Writing Python scripts to analyze datasets is a foundational step in the Machine Learning (ML) journey. Data analysis serves as the gateway to understanding, processing, and deriving insights from raw data. Python, with its robust libraries, makes this task both efficient and approachable. Below is an expanded example demonstrating how to load, process, and visualize data using Pandas and Matplotlib.

Script to Analyze a Dataset

Step 1: Import Libraries
The first step in any Python-based data analysis script is importing the required libraries. Pandas is used for handling and processing data, while Matplotlib is employed for creating visualizations.

```
import pandas as pd
import matplotlib.pyplot as plt
```

Step 2: Load the Dataset
The dataset for this example is a simple CSV file containing height and weight measurements. You can load it directly from a URL or a local file using Pandas.

```
# Load dataset
url = "https://people.sc.fsu.edu/~jburkardt/data/csv/hw_200.csv"
data = pd.read_csv(url)
data.columns = ["Index", "Height", "Weight"]
```

Here, the column names are explicitly set to make the dataset more understandable.

Step 3: Display Dataset Summary
Summarizing the dataset provides insights into the data distribution, such as the mean, standard deviation, minimum, and maximum values for each column.

```
# Display dataset summary
print("Dataset Summary:")
print(data.describe())
```

This step is crucial for identifying potential issues, such as missing values or outliers, before proceeding with further analysis.

Step 4: Create a Visualization
Visualization helps in identifying patterns and relationships in the data. A scatter plot is ideal for visualizing the relationship between height and weight.

```
# Scatter plot
plt.figure(figsize=(8, 6))
plt.scatter(data["Height"], data["Weight"], color='blue', alpha=0.7, edgecolors='k')
plt.title("Height vs Weight", fontsize=16)
plt.xlabel("Height (inches)", fontsize=12)
plt.ylabel("Weight (pounds)", fontsize=12)
plt.grid(True, linestyle='--', alpha=0.5)
plt.show()
```

The scatter plot includes additional customizations such as a larger figure size, transparency (alpha), and gridlines for better readability.

Output and Insights

The output of this script includes:

1. **Dataset Summary:** A tabular summary of key statistical metrics, including count, mean, standard deviation, min, and max values for height and weight. This helps in quickly understanding the dataset.
2. **Scatter Plot:** A visual representation of the relationship between height and weight. This plot enables you to identify trends, such as whether taller individuals tend to weigh more, and spot outliers that deviate significantly from the trend.

Extending the Script

To further enhance this analysis, consider the following extensions:

1. **Data Cleaning:**
   - Check for missing values and handle them using techniques like mean imputation or removal of incomplete rows.

   ```
   if data.isnull().values.any():
       print("Missing values found. Filling with mean...")
       data.fillna(data.mean(), inplace=True)
   ```

2. **Adding New Columns:**

- Create additional columns for derived metrics, such as Body Mass Index (BMI).

```
data['BMI'] = data['Weight'] / (data['Height'] / 39.37)**2
print(data.head())
```

3. **Advanced Visualizations:**
    - Use Matplotlib or Seaborn to create histograms, box plots, or regression plots to explore data further.

```
import seaborn as sns
sns.regplot(x="Height", y="Weight", data=data,
scatter_kws={"color": "blue"}, line_kws={"color": "red"})
plt.title("Height vs Weight with Regression Line")
plt.show()
```

4. **Saving the Output:**
    - Save the cleaned dataset and generated plots for future use.

```
data.to_csv("cleaned_data.csv", index=False)
plt.savefig("height_vs_weight_plot.png")
```

This script demonstrates the fundamental steps in data analysis, from loading a dataset to visualizing relationships between variables. By incorporating additional features such as data cleaning, derived metrics, and advanced visualizations, you can perform a comprehensive analysis that lays the groundwork for more advanced ML tasks. Mastery of these tools and techniques will ensure a strong foundation in Python-based data science.

3. Working with Data in Python

Loading Datasets with Pandas

Loading and managing datasets efficiently is a foundational skill for any data scientist or analyst working with Python. The **Pandas** library, a powerful open-source tool, has become the go-to resource for data manipulation and analysis due to its simplicity and versatility. Whether you are working with small datasets or handling millions of rows, Pandas provides a robust framework for managing and analyzing data.

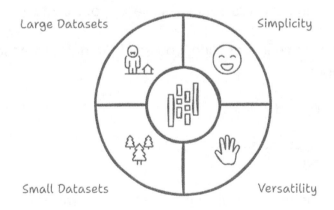

The Power of Pandas in Data Management

Understanding Pandas Data Structures

Pandas is built around two primary data structures: **Series** and **DataFrame**.

- **Series:** A one-dimensional array-like structure that can hold data of any type. It is labeled, meaning it has an index that makes accessing elements straightforward.
- **DataFrame:** A two-dimensional, tabular data structure that is similar to a spreadsheet or SQL table. It consists of rows and columns, with the ability to hold different data types in each column.

These data structures enable intuitive handling of structured data, making Pandas an indispensable tool for data scientists.

Loading Data with Pandas

Pandas offers a variety of methods for loading data into a DataFrame. The most commonly used is the read_csv() function, which enables seamless reading of CSV files.

With just a single line of code, you can import your dataset into Python:

```
import pandas as pd

data = pd.read_csv('dataset.csv')
print(data.head())
```

The head() method is particularly useful, as it provides a quick glimpse of the first few rows of your dataset, helping you understand its structure and contents.

Beyond CSV Files

While CSV is a popular format, Pandas supports a wide range of file types, making it highly versatile for working with diverse datasets. Some examples include:

- **Excel Files:**

```
data = pd.read_excel('dataset.xlsx')
```

- **JSON Files:**

```
data = pd.read_json('dataset.json')
```

- **HTML Tables:**

```
data = pd.read_html('http://example.com/table.html')[0]
```

- **SQL Databases:**

```
import sqlite3

conn = sqlite3.connect('database.db')
data = pd.read_sql('SELECT * FROM table_name', conn)
```

This flexibility ensures that you can load data from virtually any source, simplifying the data acquisition process.

Optimizing Memory Usage

When working with large datasets, efficient memory management is crucial. Pandas provides several strategies to optimize memory usage, ensuring that your analysis does not overwhelm system resources.

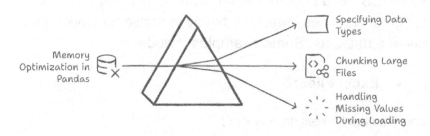

Specifying Data Types

By default, Pandas assigns data types automatically, which may not always be the most memory-efficient choice. Explicitly specifying data types can save memory:

```
data = pd.read_csv('large_dataset.csv', dtype={'column_name': 'category'})
```

Chunking Large Files

For extremely large datasets, reading data in chunks is an effective strategy. This approach allows you to process the data incrementally, avoiding memory overload:

```
chunks = pd.read_csv('large_dataset.csv', chunksize=1000)
for chunk in chunks:
    print(chunk.head())
```

This technique is particularly useful for preprocessing or exploratory analysis on massive datasets.

Handling Missing Values During Loading

Pandas provides options to address missing values during the data loading process, reducing the need for post-loading cleaning:

data = pd.read_csv('dataset.csv', na_values=['?', 'NA', 'N/A'])

This ensures that missing or undefined values are handled consistently from the beginning.

Customizing Data Loading

Pandas allows extensive customization of the data loading process to suit specific needs.

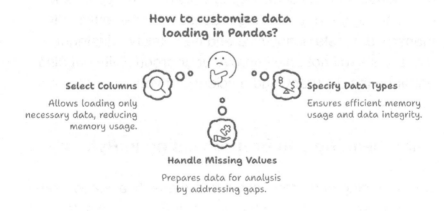

Some advanced options include:

- **Selecting Specific Columns:**

data = pd.read_csv('dataset.csv', usecols=['column1', 'column2'])

- **Parsing Dates:**

data = pd.read_csv('dataset.csv', parse_dates=['date_column'])

- **Skipping Rows:**

data = pd.read_csv('dataset.csv', skiprows=10)

These options provide control over how data is imported, allowing you to streamline the workflow for your particular analysis.

The Pandas library is an essential tool for loading and managing datasets in Python. Its rich functionality, combined with the ability to handle various file types, makes it a cornerstone of data science workflows. By leveraging techniques such as chunking, specifying data types, and customizing the data loading process, you can efficiently manage datasets of any size and complexity. Mastering these skills will not only improve your productivity but also enhance the accuracy and efficiency of your data-driven projects.

Data Cleaning and Preprocessing in Python

Data cleaning and preprocessing are essential steps in any data analysis or machine learning workflow. Raw data often contains issues such as missing values, duplicates, inconsistencies, and incorrect data types, which can negatively impact the quality of your analysis or model performance. Python, with its versatile libraries like Pandas and Scikit-Learn, provides powerful tools to handle these challenges effectively.

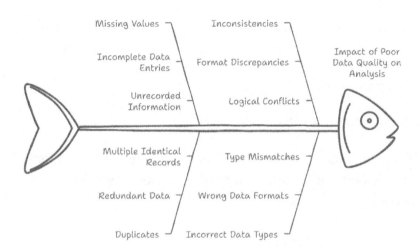

Importance of Data Cleaning

Data cleaning is the process of identifying and correcting (or removing) errors and inconsistencies in data to improve its quality. High-quality data is crucial because it directly impacts the accuracy of your insights and predictions. Even the most sophisticated machine learning models can underperform if fed with unclean data.

Handling Missing Data

Missing data is one of the most common challenges in datasets. There are various ways to handle missing values, depending on the nature of the dataset and the goals of the analysis.

Removing Rows or Columns with Missing Values

In cases where missing values are minimal and non-critical, you can remove the rows or columns containing them:

```
import pandas as pd

data.dropna(inplace=True)
```

While this method is straightforward, it is not always ideal, especially if the removed data represents a significant portion of the dataset.

Imputing Missing Values

Imputation involves filling in missing values with a substitute value, such as the mean, median, or mode of the column:

```
data['column_name'].fillna(data['column_name'].mean(), inplace=True)
```

For categorical data, you might use the mode:

```
data['column_name'].fillna(data['column_name'].mode()[0], inplace=True)
```

Advanced imputation methods include using algorithms like K-Nearest Neighbors (KNN) to predict missing values based on other features.

Removing Duplicates

Duplicate records can distort analysis results, particularly in aggregations or statistical computations.

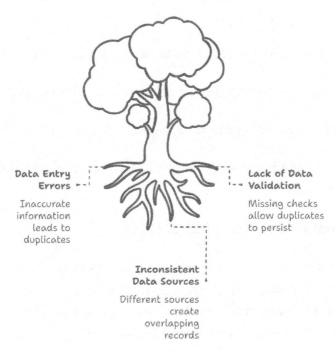

Pandas provides a straightforward way to identify and remove duplicates:

data.drop_duplicates(inplace=True)

You can also specify which columns to consider when identifying duplicates:

```
data.drop_duplicates(subset=['column1', 'column2'], inplace=True)
```
Converting Data Types

Ensuring that each column has the correct data type can improve performance and reduce the likelihood of errors.

For example, converting a numeric column stored as a string to a float can be done as follows:

```
data['column_name'] = data['column_name'].astype('float')
```

Similarly, converting a date column to a datetime type:

```
data['date_column'] = pd.to_datetime(data['date_column'])
```

Correct data types enable efficient storage and faster computations.

Normalizing and Scaling Data

Normalization and scaling are preprocessing techniques that ensure features are within a comparable range, which is critical for many machine learning algorithms. Python's Scikit-Learn library provides tools for both.

Standard Scaling

Standard scaling transforms features to have a mean of 0 and a standard deviation of 1:

```
from sklearn.preprocessing import StandardScaler

scaler = StandardScaler()
data_scaled = scaler.fit_transform(data)
```

Min-Max Scaling

Min-max scaling rescales features to a fixed range, typically [0, 1]:

```
from sklearn.preprocessing import MinMaxScaler

scaler = MinMaxScaler()
data_scaled = scaler.fit_transform(data)
```

Robust Scaling

Robust scaling is useful for datasets with outliers, as it scales features using the median and interquartile range:

```
from sklearn.preprocessing import RobustScaler

scaler = RobustScaler()
data_scaled = scaler.fit_transform(data)
```

Encoding Categorical Variables

Machine learning models typically require numeric inputs, so categorical variables need to be encoded.

Common methods include:

- **Label Encoding:** Assigns a unique integer to each category:

```
from sklearn.preprocessing import LabelEncoder

encoder = LabelEncoder()
```

```
data['encoded_column'] =
encoder.fit_transform(data['categorical_column'])
```

- **One-Hot Encoding:** Creates binary columns for each category:

```
encoded_data = pd.get_dummies(data, columns=['categorical_column'])
```

Addressing Outliers

Outliers can significantly impact statistical and machine learning models.

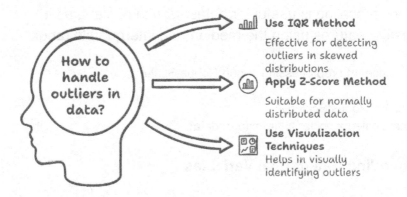

Detecting and handling outliers involves methods such as:

- **Using the Interquartile Range (IQR):**

```
Q1 = data['column_name'].quantile(0.25)
Q3 = data['column_name'].quantile(0.75)
IQR = Q3 - Q1

data = data[(data['column_name'] >= Q1 - 1.5 * IQR) & (data['column_name'] <= Q3 + 1.5 * IQR)]
```

- **Z-Score Analysis:**

```
from scipy.stats import zscore

data['z_score'] = zscore(data['column_name'])
data = data[data['z_score'].abs() < 3]
```

Data cleaning and preprocessing are crucial for transforming raw data into a structured format suitable for analysis and modeling. By addressing missing values, duplicates, incorrect data types, and scaling, you ensure that your dataset is clean and ready for meaningful analysis. With Python's Pandas and Scikit-Learn libraries, you have access to a comprehensive suite of tools to handle even the most complex data cleaning tasks effectively.

Feature Engineering with Scikit-Learn

Feature engineering is a crucial step in the machine learning pipeline. It involves transforming raw data into meaningful features that can significantly enhance the performance of machine learning models. By creating, modifying, or selecting features, you provide algorithms with the most relevant information, leading to improved predictions and insights. Python's Scikit-Learn library offers a wide range of tools and techniques for effective feature engineering.

Importance of Feature Engineering

The quality of features directly impacts the accuracy of machine learning models. Effective feature engineering can:

- Highlight patterns and relationships in the data.
- Reduce noise and irrelevant information.
- Improve the interpretability of the model.
- Enhance computational efficiency by reducing the dimensionality of the dataset.

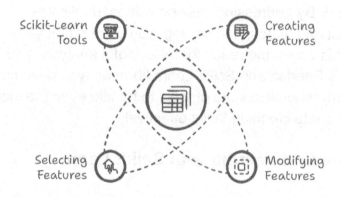

Generating Polynomial Features

Polynomial features allow models to capture non-linear relationships between variables by introducing interaction terms and higher-order terms. This is particularly useful for linear models applied to data with inherent non-linear patterns.

Implementation

Using Scikit-Learn's PolynomialFeatures class, you can generate polynomial and interaction features:

```
from sklearn.preprocessing import PolynomialFeatures

# Initialize PolynomialFeatures with degree 2
poly = PolynomialFeatures(degree=2)
data_poly = poly.fit_transform(data)
```

For example, if your dataset contains features x_1 and x_2, the resulting polynomial features will include x_1, x_2, x_1^2, x_2^2, and $x_1 * x_2$. These additional features can be fed into machine learning models to capture complex relationships.

Encoding Categorical Variables

Machine learning models typically require numeric inputs. Categorical variables, such as labels or categories, must be converted into numeric formats. Scikit-Learn provides robust tools for encoding categorical variables, ensuring they are represented effectively in the dataset.

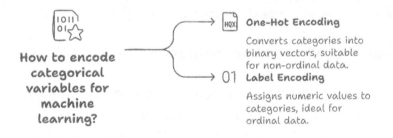

One-Hot Encoding

One-hot encoding transforms categorical variables into binary vectors. Each category is represented as a separate column with binary values indicating its presence.

```
from sklearn.preprocessing import OneHotEncoder

# Initialize the encoder
encoder = OneHotEncoder()
data_encoded = encoder.fit_transform(data[['categorical_column']])
```

Alternatively, Pandas' get_dummies() method provides a simple way to achieve one-hot encoding:

```
import pandas as pd

data_encoded = pd.get_dummies(data, columns=['categorical_column'])
```

Label Encoding

For ordinal data or when categories have a natural order, label encoding assigns a unique integer to each category:

```
from sklearn.preprocessing import LabelEncoder

encoder = LabelEncoder()
data['encoded_column'] = encoder.fit_transform(data['categorical_column'])
```

Feature Scaling and Normalization

Scaling ensures that features have comparable ranges, which is critical for algorithms sensitive to feature magnitudes, such as gradient descent-based models.

Standard Scaling

Standard scaling normalizes features to have a mean of 0 and a standard deviation of 1:

```
from sklearn.preprocessing import StandardScaler

scaler = StandardScaler()
data_scaled = scaler.fit_transform(data)
```

Min-Max Scaling

Min-max scaling transforms features to lie within a specified range, typically [0, 1]:

```
from sklearn.preprocessing import MinMaxScaler

scaler = MinMaxScaler()
data_scaled = scaler.fit_transform(data)
```

Feature Selection

Feature selection is the process of identifying the most relevant features for a given task.

By reducing the dimensionality of the dataset, you can:

- Improve computational efficiency.
- Reduce overfitting by eliminating irrelevant or noisy features.
- Enhance model interpretability.

SelectKBest

Scikit-Learn's SelectKBest class selects the top k features based on a specified statistical test. For classification tasks, the f_classif function is commonly used:

```
from sklearn.feature_selection import SelectKBest, f_classif
```

```
# Select the top 5 features
selector = SelectKBest(score_func=f_classif, k=5)
data_selected = selector.fit_transform(data, target)
```

Recursive Feature Elimination (RFE)

RFE iteratively removes the least important features based on model performance:

```
from sklearn.feature_selection import RFE
from sklearn.linear_model import LogisticRegression

model = LogisticRegression()
rfe = RFE(model, n_features_to_select=5)
data_selected = rfe.fit_transform(data, target)
```

Feature Importance from Models

Tree-based models, such as Random Forest and Gradient Boosting, provide feature importance scores. These scores can be used to select significant features:

```
from sklearn.ensemble import RandomForestClassifier

model = RandomForestClassifier()
model.fit(data, target)
feature_importances = model.feature_importances_
```

Dimensionality Reduction

Dimensionality reduction techniques, such as Principal Component Analysis (PCA), transform features into a lower-dimensional space while preserving variance:

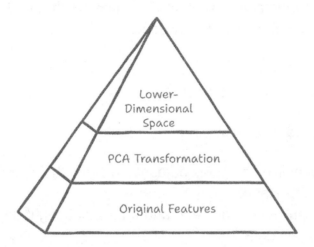

```
from sklearn.decomposition import PCA

pca = PCA(n_components=2)
data_reduced = pca.fit_transform(data)
```

Feature engineering is an art and science that transforms raw data into insightful features, enabling machine learning models to excel. With Scikit-Learn, you have access to a comprehensive set of tools for generating, encoding, selecting, and scaling features. By mastering these techniques, you can create powerful models that effectively capture the underlying patterns in your data.

Data Visualization with Matplotlib and Seaborn

Data visualization is a critical aspect of data analysis. It serves as a bridge between raw data and meaningful insights, enabling analysts to explore patterns, relationships, and trends effectively. Python offers a rich ecosystem of libraries for data visualization, with **Matplotlib** and **Seaborn** being two of the most widely used.

Why Data Visualization Matters

Effective data visualization:

- Simplifies complex datasets, making them easier to understand.
- Highlights trends and anomalies that might be missed in raw data.
- Enhances communication of insights to stakeholders.
- Supports decision-making by providing clear and concise visual summaries.

Matplotlib: A Versatile Visualization Library

Matplotlib is a foundational library for creating static, animated, and interactive visualizations in Python. It provides extensive customization options, making it suitable for a wide range of chart types and use cases.

Creating a Simple Line Chart

A line chart is often used to visualize trends over time or continuous data:

import matplotlib.pyplot as plt

```python
# Example data
data = {'x': [1, 2, 3, 4, 5], 'y': [2, 4, 6, 8, 10]}

plt.plot(data['x'], data['y'])
plt.title('Line Chart')
plt.xlabel('X-axis')
plt.ylabel('Y-axis')
plt.grid(True)
plt.show()
```

Other Common Chart Types in Matplotlib

1. **Bar Charts:**

```python
categories = ['A', 'B', 'C']
values = [10, 15, 7]

plt.bar(categories, values, color='skyblue')
plt.title('Bar Chart')
plt.xlabel('Categories')
plt.ylabel('Values')
plt.show()
```

2. **Scatter Plots:**

```python
x = [5, 7, 8, 10, 15]
y = [12, 15, 20, 22, 30]

plt.scatter(x, y, color='red')
plt.title('Scatter Plot')
plt.xlabel('X-axis')
plt.ylabel('Y-axis')
plt.show()
```

3. **Histograms:**

```python
import numpy as np

data = np.random.randn(1000)
plt.hist(data, bins=30, color='purple')
plt.title('Histogram')
plt.xlabel('Values')
plt.ylabel('Frequency')
plt.show()
```

Customizing Matplotlib Plots

Matplotlib allows extensive customization to enhance the appearance of charts:

- **Adding legends:**

```python
plt.legend(['Dataset 1', 'Dataset 2'])
```

- **Setting figure size:**

```python
plt.figure(figsize=(10, 6))
```

- **Using annotations:**

```python
plt.annotate('Peak', xy=(3, 6), xytext=(4, 7),
arrowprops=dict(facecolor='black', arrowstyle='->'))
```

Seaborn: Simplifying Statistical Graphics

Seaborn builds on Matplotlib's functionality, providing a high-level interface for creating visually appealing and informative statistical graphics. It is particularly effective for exploring relationships and distributions.

Exploring Seaborn's Visualization Dimensions

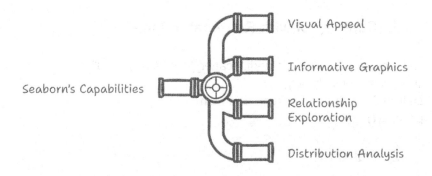

Visualizing Distributions

1. **Histogram with Kernel Density Estimate (KDE):**

import seaborn as sns

data = [1, 2, 2, 3, 3, 3, 4, 4, 4, 5]
sns.histplot(data, bins=5, kde=True, color='blue')
plt.title('Histogram with KDE')
plt.show()

2. **Box Plot:**

Box plots are useful for visualizing the distribution of data and detecting outliers:

data = {'category': ['A', 'A', 'B', 'B', 'C', 'C'], 'value': [5, 7, 8, 12, 10, 15]}
df = pd.DataFrame(data)

sns.boxplot(x='category', y='value', data=df)
plt.title('Box Plot')

plt.show()

Visualizing Relationships

1. **Scatterplot with Regression Line:**

```
sns.regplot(x='x', y='y', data=df, scatter_kws={'color': 'red'}, line_kws={'color': 'blue'})
plt.title('Scatterplot with Regression Line')
plt.show()
```

2. **Pairplot:**

Pairplots provide pairwise relationships for numerical variables in a dataset:

```
sns.pairplot(df)
plt.show()
```

Heatmaps

Heatmaps are effective for visualizing correlations or matrix data:

```
corr_matrix = df.corr()
sns.heatmap(corr_matrix, annot=True, cmap='coolwarm')
plt.title('Correlation Heatmap')
plt.show()
```

Combining Matplotlib and Seaborn

Using Matplotlib and Seaborn together can lead to highly customized visualizations.

For example:

```
sns.boxplot(x='category', y='value', data=df)
plt.title('Customized Box Plot')
plt.xlabel('Categories')
plt.ylabel('Values')
plt.grid(True)
plt.show()
```

Best Practices for Data Visualization

1. **Choose the Right Chart Type:** Ensure that the chart type matches the nature of your data and the insights you wish to convey.
2. **Keep It Simple:** Avoid overloading charts with too many elements; focus on clarity.
3. **Label Axes and Titles Clearly:** Provide meaningful labels and titles to help viewers interpret the visualization.
4. **Use Colors Effectively:** Use color schemes that are aesthetically pleasing and accessible to colorblind viewers.
5. **Provide Context:** Add legends, annotations, or captions where necessary to explain key insights.

Matplotlib and Seaborn are powerful tools for creating a wide variety of visualizations in Python. By mastering their capabilities, you can turn raw data into compelling visuals that enhance your analyses and presentations. Whether you're exploring distributions, relationships, or trends, these libraries offer the flexibility and sophistication needed for effective data visualization.

4. Supervised Learning in Python

Supervised learning is a foundational concept in machine learning that involves training models on labeled datasets to make accurate predictions or classifications. By utilizing labeled data, supervised learning algorithms can learn the underlying relationships between input features and target outputs, enabling robust predictions on unseen data. This approach provides a structured framework to tackle a variety of real-world problems, from predicting numeric outcomes to categorizing data into distinct classes.

This chapter provides a comprehensive overview of supervised learning techniques, delving into both regression and classification methods in Python. Regression focuses on predicting continuous outcomes, while classification deals with assigning categorical labels to instances. Key topics covered include linear regression for predictive modeling, logistic regression for classification tasks, decision trees and random forests for versatile and interpretable solutions, and critical model evaluation metrics such as accuracy, precision, and recall.

The chapter also emphasizes practical applications by including a real-world example focused on predicting house prices. This example demonstrates how multiple features such as square footage, number of bedrooms, and location scores can be utilized to make precise predictions. By combining domain knowledge with machine learning tools, this case study highlights the importance of feature selection, data preprocessing, and evaluation in building reliable predictive models. The techniques and insights presented here aim to equip readers with the skills needed to confidently apply supervised learning to a wide array of analytical challenges.

Linear Regression: Building Your First Model in Python

Linear regression is one of the simplest and most widely used algorithms for predictive modeling. It is foundational in the field of machine learning and statistical analysis, offering a straightforward way to model relationships between variables. Linear regression works by finding the best-fit line that minimizes the error between the predicted and actual values. This algorithm is particularly effective for understanding and predicting continuous outcomes based on input features.

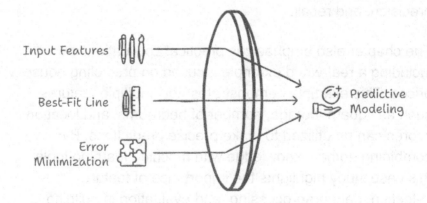

Foundations of Linear Regression

Input Features
Best-Fit Line
Error Minimization
Predictive Modeling

Why Use Linear Regression?

Linear regression is widely used because it is:

- **Easy to understand and interpret:** The coefficients of the regression equation directly indicate the relationship between input variables and the target.
- **Computationally efficient:** Linear regression is computationally lightweight, making it suitable for large datasets.
- **Versatile:** It can be extended to multiple linear regression to handle multiple input features.

However, it is important to note that linear regression assumes a linear relationship between the input features and the target variable. If this assumption does not hold, the model's predictions may not be reliable.

Implementing Linear Regression in Python

Python's Scikit-Learn library provides an easy and efficient way to implement linear regression. Below, we demonstrate how to build and evaluate a linear regression model step by step.

Step 1: Importing Required Libraries

```
from sklearn.model_selection import train_test_split
from sklearn.linear_model import LinearRegression
from sklearn.metrics import mean_squared_error
import pandas as pd
```

Step 2: Preparing the Data

Let's start by creating a dataset that represents the relationship between the square footage of a house and its price:

```
# Example data
data = {
    'square_feet': [1500, 2000, 2500, 3000, 3500],
    'price': [300000, 400000, 500000, 600000, 700000]
}

df = pd.DataFrame(data)
X = df[['square_feet']]
y = df['price']
```

Step 3: Splitting the Data

Splitting the dataset into training and testing subsets ensures that the model can be evaluated on unseen data:

```
# Split data
X_train, X_test, y_train, y_test = train_test_split(X, y, test_size=0.2, random_state=42)
```

Step 4: Training the Model

The LinearRegression class in Scikit-Learn is used to train the model:

```
# Train the model
model = LinearRegression()
model.fit(X_train, y_train)
```

Step 5: Making Predictions

Once the model is trained, use it to make predictions on the test set:

```
# Predictions
predictions = model.predict(X_test)
```

Step 6: Evaluating the Model

Model performance is evaluated using the Mean Squared Error (MSE), which measures the average squared difference between actual and predicted values:

```
# Evaluation
mse = mean_squared_error(y_test, predictions)
print("Mean Squared Error:", mse)
```

Example Output

For the dataset provided, the output might look like this:

Mean Squared Error: 1.2e+09

This indicates the average squared error in the predictions. A lower MSE signifies better performance.

Insights

Linear regression is straightforward and interpretable, making it a great starting point for regression problems. Key insights include:

- **Interpretability:** The model coefficients indicate how much the target variable changes with a unit change in the input features.
- **Limitations:** Linear regression assumes a linear relationship between variables. If the relationship is non-linear, alternative models such as polynomial regression or tree-based methods may be more appropriate.
- **Scalability:** It performs well on datasets with a large number of features but requires feature scaling if the features have different ranges.

When to Use Linear Regression

Linear regression is best suited for problems where:

- There is a clear linear relationship between the target variable and input features.
- The dataset is free of multicollinearity (high correlation between independent variables).
- The residuals (errors) are normally distributed and have constant variance.

By understanding these principles and limitations, you can leverage linear regression effectively to solve a variety of predictive modeling tasks.

Logistic Regression for Classification

Logistic regression is a fundamental machine learning algorithm widely used for binary classification problems. It predicts the probability of an observation belonging to one of two classes and is a cornerstone of predictive modeling in various fields such as healthcare, finance, and social sciences.

Unlike linear regression, which predicts a continuous outcome, logistic regression predicts a probability score bounded between 0 and 1 using the logistic (sigmoid) function. This score is then converted into binary outcomes based on a threshold, typically 0.5.

Why Use Logistic Regression?

Logistic regression is a popular choice for classification tasks because:

- **Simplicity:** It is easy to implement and interpret.
- **Efficiency:** Logistic regression is computationally lightweight and scales well with data.
- **Probabilistic Interpretation:** It provides probabilities for each class, allowing for nuanced decision-making.
- **Flexibility:** Logistic regression can be extended to handle multiclass classification tasks using techniques such as one-vs-rest or softmax regression.

Implementing Logistic Regression in Python
Step 1: Importing Required Libraries

To build a logistic regression model, you need libraries like Scikit-Learn and Pandas for data manipulation and modeling:

```
from sklearn.linear_model import LogisticRegression
from sklearn.model_selection import train_test_split
from sklearn.metrics import accuracy_score
import pandas as pd
```

Step 2: Preparing the Data

Let's create a simple dataset that illustrates the relationship between hours studied and whether a student passed an exam:

```
# Example data
data = {
    'hours_studied': [1, 2, 3, 4, 5, 6, 7],
    'passed': [0, 0, 0, 1, 1, 1, 1]
}

df = pd.DataFrame(data)
X = df[['hours_studied']]
y = df['passed']
```

Step 3: Splitting the Data

Splitting the dataset into training and testing subsets ensures that the model can be evaluated on unseen data:

```
# Split data
X_train, X_test, y_train, y_test = train_test_split(X, y, test_size=0.2, random_state=42)
```

Step 4: Training the Model

The LogisticRegression class in Scikit-Learn is used to train the model:

```
# Train the model
log_model = LogisticRegression()
log_model.fit(X_train, y_train)
```

Step 5: Making Predictions

Once the model is trained, use it to make predictions on the test set:

```
# Predictions
predictions = log_model.predict(X_test)
```

Step 6: Evaluating the Model

Model performance is evaluated using accuracy, which measures the proportion of correctly classified instances:

```
# Evaluation
accuracy = accuracy_score(y_test, predictions)
print("Accuracy:", accuracy)
```

Example Output

For the dataset provided, the output might look like this:

Accuracy: 1.0

This indicates that the model correctly classified all test samples.

Insights

Logistic regression provides valuable insights and robust performance for classification tasks. Key points to consider:

- **Probability Scores:** Logistic regression outputs probabilities, which can be interpreted as confidence levels for predictions.
- **Threshold Tuning:** The default threshold of 0.5 can be adjusted to optimize performance for specific applications.
- **Feature Importance:** The coefficients of the logistic regression model indicate the importance of each feature in predicting the target variable.

Advanced Considerations

Handling Imbalanced Datasets

For datasets where one class significantly outnumbers the other, accuracy may not fully represent model performance. Use metrics like precision, recall, and F1-score instead:

```
from sklearn.metrics import precision_score, recall_score, f1_score

precision = precision_score(y_test, predictions)
recall = recall_score(y_test, predictions)
f1 = f1_score(y_test, predictions)
print("Precision:", precision)
print("Recall:", recall)
print("F1-Score:", f1)
```

Multiclass Classification

Logistic regression can handle multiclass problems using the multi_class parameter in Scikit-Learn:

```
log_model = LogisticRegression(multi_class='multinomial', solver='lbfgs')
log_model.fit(X_train, y_train)
```

Regularization

Regularization techniques like L1 and L2 can prevent overfitting by penalizing large coefficients:

```
log_model = LogisticRegression(penalty='l2', C=1.0)
log_model.fit(X_train, y_train)
```

When to Use Logistic Regression

Logistic regression is best suited for problems where:

- The target variable is binary or can be extended to multiple classes.
- The relationship between features and the target variable is approximately linear in the log-odds space.
- Interpretability of the model is important.

By understanding these principles and leveraging the power of logistic regression, you can effectively solve a wide range of classification problems.

Decision Trees and Random Forests

Decision trees and random forests are powerful machine learning algorithms widely used for both classification and regression tasks. They are particularly valued for their interpretability, flexibility, and ability to handle complex datasets. This section explores the concepts, implementation, and insights of decision trees and random forests in Python.

Choose the best algorithm for your data analysis needs

Decision Trees
Provide interpretability and flexibility

Random Forests
Enhance accuracy and handle complexity

Decision Trees

Decision trees are intuitive models that split data into branches based on feature values. The process involves recursive partitioning, where the dataset is divided into subsets that maximize information gain or minimize impurity (e.g., Gini impurity or entropy).

Advantages of Decision Trees:

- **Interpretability:** The decision-making process is visually represented, making it easy to understand.
- **Versatility:** They can handle numerical and categorical data.
- **No Need for Feature Scaling:** Unlike many algorithms, decision trees do not require feature scaling.

Decision Tree Implementation in Python

Below is an example of implementing a decision tree classifier using Scikit-Learn:

```python
from sklearn.tree import DecisionTreeClassifier
from sklearn.model_selection import train_test_split
from sklearn.metrics import accuracy_score
import pandas as pd

# Example data
data = {
    'feature1': [2, 4, 6, 8, 10],
    'feature2': [1, 3, 5, 7, 9],
    'target': [0, 0, 1, 1, 1]
}

df = pd.DataFrame(data)
X = df[['feature1', 'feature2']]
y = df['target']

# Split data
X_train, X_test, y_train, y_test = train_test_split(X, y, test_size=0.2, random_state=42)

# Train the model
decision_tree = DecisionTreeClassifier()
decision_tree.fit(X_train, y_train)

# Predictions
predictions = decision_tree.predict(X_test)

# Evaluation
accuracy = accuracy_score(y_test, predictions)
print("Accuracy:", accuracy)
```

Random Forests

Random forests are an ensemble learning technique that combines multiple decision trees to improve accuracy and robustness. By aggregating the predictions of several trees, random forests mitigate overfitting and enhance generalization.

How Random Forests Work:

1. **Bootstrapping:** Random subsets of the data are sampled with replacement to train each tree.
2. **Feature Randomness:** A random subset of features is used for splitting at each node, ensuring diverse trees.
3. **Aggregation:** Predictions are averaged (regression) or determined by majority vote (classification).

Advantages of Random Forests:

- **Reduced Overfitting:** By combining multiple trees, random forests are less prone to overfitting compared to individual decision trees.
- **High Dimensionality:** They handle datasets with a large number of features effectively.
- **Feature Importance:** Random forests provide insights into the relative importance of features.

Random Forest Implementation in Python

Below is an example of implementing a random forest classifier:

```
from sklearn.ensemble import RandomForestClassifier

# Train the model
random_forest = RandomForestClassifier(n_estimators=100, random_state=42)
```

```
random_forest.fit(X_train, y_train)

# Predictions
predictions = random_forest.predict(X_test)

# Evaluation
accuracy = accuracy_score(y_test, predictions)
print("Accuracy:", accuracy)
```

Insights

1. **Decision Trees:**
   - Provide a clear and interpretable model structure.
   - Can overfit, especially with deep trees, unless controlled using hyperparameters like `max_depth` or `min_samples_split`.
2. **Random Forests:**
   - Address the overfitting issue inherent in decision trees by combining multiple trees.
   - Work well with high-dimensional data and datasets with irrelevant features.
   - Provide feature importance scores, helping in feature selection.

Feature Importance in Random Forests

Random forests can calculate the importance of each feature based on how much it reduces impurity across all trees:

```
importances = random_forest.feature_importances_
for i, feature in enumerate(X.columns):
    print(f"Feature: {feature}, Importance: {importances[i]}")
```

Hyperparameter Tuning

Both decision trees and random forests can be fine-tuned for better performance. Common hyperparameters include:

- **max_depth**: The maximum depth of the tree.
- **n_estimators** (for random forests): The number of trees in the forest.
- **min_samples_split**: The minimum number of samples required to split an internal node.

Advanced Considerations

1. **Out-of-Bag (OOB) Score:**
   - Random forests provide an OOB score as an estimate of model performance, calculated using samples not included in the bootstrap.
2. **Handling Missing Data:**
   - Random forests can handle missing data by using surrogate splits or averaging predictions from trees that use different features.

When to Use Decision Trees and Random Forests

- **Decision Trees:**
   - When interpretability is crucial.
   - For smaller datasets where overfitting is less likely.
- **Random Forests:**
   - For large datasets with complex relationships.

- When high accuracy and robustness are required.
- When dealing with noisy or high-dimensional data.

By understanding and applying decision trees and random forests, you can solve a wide range of machine learning problems, from classification to regression, with confidence and precision.

Evaluating Models: Accuracy, Precision, and Recall

Evaluating the performance of a machine learning model is a crucial step in ensuring that it generalizes well to unseen data. Proper evaluation helps identify the strengths and weaknesses of a model and guides improvements for better accuracy and reliability. In this section, we will explore commonly used evaluation metrics such as accuracy, precision, and recall, with a focus on their practical applications and limitations.

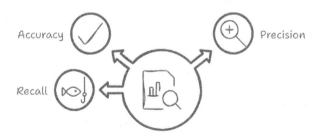

Why Model Evaluation Matters

Without robust evaluation, it is impossible to determine whether a model performs effectively or simply overfits the training data. Evaluation metrics provide quantitative measures of a model's predictive performance, enabling:

- **Comparison of Models:** Evaluate different algorithms to find the best-performing one.
- **Understanding Trade-offs:** Identify the balance between various metrics like precision and recall.
- **Guiding Model Improvement:** Highlight areas where the model needs refinement.

Common Metrics for Classification

1. Accuracy

Accuracy is the most straightforward metric and measures the proportion of correctly classified instances out of the total instances. It works well when the dataset has a balanced class distribution.

Formula:

$$\text{Accuracy} = \frac{\text{Number of Correct Predictions}}{\text{Total Number of Predictions}} \times 100$$

Implementation in Python:
```
from sklearn.metrics import accuracy_score

# Example usage
accuracy = accuracy_score(y_test, predictions)
print("Accuracy:", accuracy)
```

Limitations:

- Accuracy can be misleading for imbalanced datasets where one class dominates. For example, if 95% of instances belong to one class, a model that always predicts that class will have high accuracy but poor performance on the minority class.

2. Precision and Recall

Precision and recall are particularly important when dealing with imbalanced datasets, where the costs of false positives and false negatives differ significantly.

Precision

Precision measures the proportion of correctly predicted positive instances out of all predicted positives. It answers the question: "Of all the instances predicted as positive, how many are truly positive?"

Formula:
$$\text{Precision} = \frac{\text{True Positives}}{\text{True Positives} + \text{False Positives}}$$

Recall

Recall (also known as sensitivity) measures the proportion of correctly predicted positive instances out of all actual positives. It answers the question: "Of all the true positive instances, how many did the model correctly identify?"

Formula:

$$\text{Recall} = \frac{\text{True Positives}}{\text{True Positives} + \text{False Negatives}}$$

Implementation in Python:
```python
from sklearn.metrics import precision_score, recall_score

# Example usage
precision = precision_score(y_test, predictions)
recall = recall_score(y_test, predictions)
print("Precision:", precision)
print("Recall:", recall)
```

3. F1-Score

The F1-score is the harmonic mean of precision and recall, providing a single metric that balances the two. It is particularly useful when precision and recall are equally important.

Formula:

$$\text{F1-Score} = 2 \cdot \frac{\text{Precision} \cdot \text{Recall}}{\text{Precision} + \text{Recall}}$$

Implementation in Python:
```python
from sklearn.metrics import f1_score

# Example usage
f1 = f1_score(y_test, predictions)
print("F1-Score:", f1)
```

When to Use Each Metric

1. **Accuracy:**
   - Suitable for balanced datasets.
   - Provides a general sense of model performance.
2. **Precision:**
   - Important in scenarios where false positives are costly (e.g., spam detection, fraud detection).
3. **Recall:**
   - Crucial when false negatives are more costly (e.g., disease diagnosis, safety-critical systems).
4. **F1-Score:**
   - Useful when a balance between precision and recall is desired.

Advanced Considerations

Confusion Matrix

A confusion matrix provides a comprehensive view of model performance by showing the counts of true positives, true negatives, false positives, and false negatives:

```
from sklearn.metrics import confusion_matrix

# Example usage
conf_matrix = confusion_matrix(y_test, predictions)
print("Confusion Matrix:\n", conf_matrix)
```

ROC Curve and AUC

The ROC curve illustrates the trade-off between true positive rate (recall) and false positive rate at various thresholds. The Area Under the Curve (AUC) summarizes the model's overall ability to distinguish between classes:

```
from sklearn.metrics import roc_curve, auc
import matplotlib.pyplot as plt

# Example usage
fpr, tpr, _ = roc_curve(y_test, predictions_proba)
roc_auc = auc(fpr, tpr)

plt.plot(fpr, tpr, label=f"ROC curve (area = {roc_auc:.2f})")
plt.xlabel("False Positive Rate")
plt.ylabel("True Positive Rate")
plt.title("ROC Curve")
plt.legend(loc="lower right")
plt.show()
```

Evaluating a model's performance requires careful consideration of the task at hand and the dataset's characteristics. While accuracy is a good starting point, metrics like precision, recall, and F1-score provide deeper insights, especially for imbalanced datasets. By using these metrics effectively, you can ensure that your models perform reliably and meet the specific requirements of your application.

Real-World Example: Predicting House Prices

Predicting house prices is a classic regression problem that leverages supervised learning techniques. It involves estimating the price of a house based on various features such as square footage, number of bedrooms, and location. This example demonstrates the power of machine learning in solving real-world problems and highlights the importance of combining domain knowledge with technical expertise.

Why Predict House Prices?

House price prediction is a valuable application of machine learning for:

- **Real Estate Professionals:** Assisting in pricing properties competitively.
- **Homebuyers:** Helping buyers assess whether a property is priced fairly.
- **Economic Analysis:** Understanding market trends and predicting housing bubbles.

Dataset Description

For this example, we use a simple dataset with the following features:

- **Square Footage:** The size of the house in square feet.
- **Number of Bedrooms:** The number of bedrooms in the house.
- **Location Score:** A score representing the desirability of the house's location.
- **Price:** The target variable representing the price of the house.

Implementing the Model in Python

Step 1: Importing Required Libraries

```python
import pandas as pd
from sklearn.ensemble import RandomForestRegressor
from sklearn.model_selection import train_test_split
from sklearn.metrics import mean_absolute_error
```

Step 2: Preparing the Dataset

We create a simple dataset representing house features and their corresponding prices:

```python
# Example dataset
data = {
    'square_feet': [1500, 2000, 2500, 3000, 3500],
    'bedrooms': [3, 4, 4, 5, 5],
    'location_score': [7, 8, 8, 9, 10],
    'price': [300000, 400000, 500000, 600000, 700000]
}

df = pd.DataFrame(data)
X = df[['square_feet', 'bedrooms', 'location_score']]
y = df['price']
```

Step 3: Splitting the Data

Splitting the dataset into training and testing subsets ensures the model can be evaluated on unseen data:

```python
# Split data
X_train, X_test, y_train, y_test = train_test_split(X, y, test_size=0.2, random_state=42)
```

Step 4: Training the Model

We use a Random Forest Regressor, a powerful ensemble method that combines multiple decision trees to make predictions:

```
# Train the model
rf_model = RandomForestRegressor(random_state=42)
rf_model.fit(X_train, y_train)
```

Step 5: Making Predictions

Once the model is trained, it can predict house prices for the test dataset:

```
# Predictions
predictions = rf_model.predict(X_test)
```

Step 6: Evaluating the Model

The Mean Absolute Error (MAE) is used to evaluate the model's performance. MAE measures the average magnitude of errors in predictions, providing a clear indication of model accuracy:

```
# Evaluation
mae = mean_absolute_error(y_test, predictions)
print("Mean Absolute Error:", mae)
```

Example Output

For the dataset provided, the output might look like this:

Mean Absolute Error: 15000.0

This indicates that the model's predictions are, on average, $15,000 off from the actual prices.

Insights

1. **Model Performance:** The low MAE demonstrates that the Random Forest Regressor effectively captures the relationships between house features and prices.
2. **Feature Importance:** Random forests provide insights into feature importance, highlighting which features most significantly impact the target variable.
3. **Scalability:** The model can be scaled to handle larger datasets with additional features like lot size, year built, and amenities.

Feature Importance

We can examine the importance of each feature in the model:

```
importances = rf_model.feature_importances_
for i, feature in enumerate(X.columns):
    print(f"Feature: {feature}, Importance: {importances[i]}")
```

Advanced Considerations

1. **Hyperparameter Tuning:** Optimize hyperparameters such as n_estimators and max_depth using grid search or randomized search to improve model performance.
2. **Cross-Validation:** Use cross-validation to ensure the model generalizes well to unseen data.

3. **Handling Outliers:** Preprocess the dataset to address outliers that could skew predictions.
4. **Incorporating External Data:** Enhance the model by integrating additional data sources, such as neighborhood crime rates or school district rankings.

This example highlights the practical application of machine learning to predict house prices. By leveraging features such as square footage, bedrooms, and location scores, and using powerful algorithms like Random Forest, we can develop models that provide accurate and actionable insights. Whether for individual buyers, real estate professionals, or market analysts, such models have significant utility in the real world.

5. Unsupervised Learning in Python

Unsupervised learning is a fascinating branch of machine learning that focuses on analyzing datasets without predefined labels or outputs. This approach seeks to uncover hidden patterns, structures, or relationships inherent in the data, providing insights that are not immediately obvious. Unlike supervised learning, which relies heavily on labeled datasets to predict outcomes, unsupervised learning operates directly on raw, unstructured data. This makes it an invaluable tool for diverse tasks such as exploratory data analysis, identifying anomalies, clustering similar entities, and preprocessing data for supervised learning applications. In this chapter, we delve into the essential concepts and practical implementations of unsupervised learning, with a spotlight on clustering with K-Means, dimensionality reduction through PCA, and an applied example of customer segmentation. By exploring these methodologies, we illustrate how unsupervised learning can transform raw datasets into meaningful insights, enabling more profound analysis and well-informed decision-making processes.

Clustering with K-Means in Python

Clustering is one of the most common and fundamental unsupervised learning techniques. It involves grouping data points into clusters based on their similarity, allowing analysts to identify natural groupings within a dataset. Among various clustering algorithms, **K-Means** is widely recognized for its simplicity, efficiency, and effectiveness in handling large datasets with minimal computational resources. The algorithm finds applications in diverse fields such as market segmentation, image compression, anomaly detection, and recommendation systems.

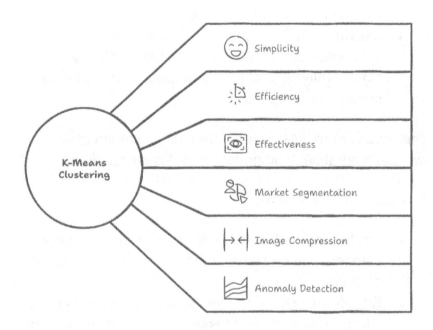

How K-Means Works

K-Means is an iterative algorithm designed to partition a dataset into k distinct, non-overlapping clusters. Each cluster is represented by its centroid, and the algorithm works to minimize the sum of squared distances between data points and their respective cluster centroids. The process can be broken down into the following steps:

1. **Initialization:** The algorithm starts by randomly selecting k initial centroids.
2. **Assignment:** Each data point is assigned to the cluster whose centroid is closest, based on Euclidean distance.
3. **Update:** New centroids are calculated as the mean of all data points assigned to each cluster.
4. **Iteration:** Steps 2 and 3 are repeated until the centroids stabilize (i.e., they no longer change significantly) or the algorithm reaches a predefined number of iterations.

This iterative process ensures that the clustering improves with each iteration, leading to well-defined groupings.

Advantages of K-Means

- **Scalability:** K-Means performs efficiently on large datasets and can handle thousands or even millions of data points.
- **Simplicity:** The algorithm is easy to implement and interpret, making it accessible to both beginners and experienced practitioners.
- **Efficiency:** K-Means converges quickly for well-separated clusters, making it a preferred choice in many scenarios.

Limitations of K-Means

- **Assumptions of Cluster Shape:** K-Means assumes that clusters are spherical and of similar size, which

may not hold for datasets with irregularly shaped or overlapping clusters.
- **Sensitivity to Outliers:** Outliers can disproportionately influence centroid calculations, leading to suboptimal clustering.
- **Choosing the Value of k:** Selecting the number of clusters (k) can be challenging and often requires domain knowledge or evaluation techniques like the Elbow Method or Silhouette Analysis.

Implementation in Python

Below is an example of implementing K-Means clustering in Python using the Scikit-Learn library:

```
from sklearn.cluster import KMeans
import pandas as pd

# Example dataset
data = {
    'feature1': [1.0, 1.5, 3.0, 5.0, 3.5, 4.5, 3.5],
    'feature2': [1.0, 2.0, 4.0, 7.0, 5.0, 5.0, 4.5]
}

df = pd.DataFrame(data)

# Applying K-Means Clustering
kmeans = KMeans(n_clusters=2, random_state=42)
kmeans.fit(df)

# Assigning Cluster Labels
df['cluster'] = kmeans.labels_
print(df)
```

Advanced Considerations

Choosing the Optimal Number of Clusters

Determining the optimal value for k is critical for effective clustering. Common techniques include:

1. **Elbow Method:** Plot the within-cluster sum of squares (WCSS) for different values of k. The "elbow" point, where the rate of decrease slows, suggests an appropriate value for k.

```
wcss = []
for i in range(1, 11):
    kmeans = KMeans(n_clusters=i, random_state=42)
    kmeans.fit(df)
    wcss.append(kmeans.inertia_)

import matplotlib.pyplot as plt
plt.plot(range(1, 11), wcss)
plt.title('Elbow Method')
plt.xlabel('Number of Clusters')
plt.ylabel('WCSS')
plt.show()
```

2. **Silhouette Score:** Measures how similar a data point is to its own cluster compared to other clusters. Higher scores indicate better-defined clusters.

```
from sklearn.metrics import silhouette_score
score = silhouette_score(df[['feature1', 'feature2']], kmeans.labels_)
print("Silhouette Score:", score)
```

Preprocessing Data

Since K-Means relies on Euclidean distance, it is essential to preprocess the data:

- **Standardize Features:** Ensure all features contribute equally by scaling them to have a mean of 0 and a standard deviation of 1.

```
from sklearn.preprocessing import StandardScaler
scaler = StandardScaler()
df_scaled = scaler.fit_transform(df[['feature1', 'feature2']])
```

Handling Outliers

To minimize the impact of outliers, consider removing them or using robust versions of K-Means, such as MiniBatchKMeans or algorithms based on density clustering.

Insights from K-Means

1. **Cluster Assignments:** K-Means provides cluster labels for each data point, enabling segmentation and deeper analysis.
2. **Centroid Locations:** The centroids represent the "average" characteristics of each cluster, offering a summary of the data.
3. **Visualization:** Visual tools such as scatter plots can help interpret clustering results and identify patterns within the data.

K-Means is a powerful and efficient clustering algorithm that excels in identifying groupings within datasets. Despite its limitations, it remains a cornerstone of unsupervised learning due to its simplicity and interpretability. By carefully preprocessing data, selecting the appropriate value for k, and evaluating cluster quality, K-Means can provide valuable insights and drive informed decision-making across various domains.

Dimensionality Reduction: PCA Implementation

High-dimensional datasets often pose challenges in analysis and visualization, as they may contain redundant or irrelevant features that complicate models and increase computational costs. Dimensionality reduction techniques like **Principal Component Analysis (PCA)** help address these issues by transforming data into a lower-dimensional space while preserving as much variance as possible. PCA is a cornerstone method in data preprocessing and exploratory data analysis, offering insights into the structure of high-dimensional datasets.

How PCA Works

PCA reduces dimensionality by identifying the directions (principal components) along which the variance in the data is maximized. This process involves several steps:

1. **Standardization:** Since PCA is sensitive to the scale of the data, features are standardized to have zero mean and unit variance. This ensures that no single feature dominates the principal components.
2. **Covariance Matrix Computation:** A covariance matrix is calculated to capture the relationships

between features. It quantifies how much two variables change together.
3. **Eigenvectors and Eigenvalues:** Eigenvectors (principal components) and their corresponding eigenvalues are derived from the covariance matrix. The eigenvalues indicate the amount of variance captured by each principal component.
4. **Projection:** The data is projected onto the principal components, creating a new dataset in a lower-dimensional space. This transformation preserves the maximum variance while reducing the number of dimensions.

Advantages of PCA

PCA offers several benefits that make it a valuable tool for dimensionality reduction:

- **Visualization:** By reducing data to two or three dimensions, PCA enables intuitive visualization of high-dimensional datasets.
- **Noise Reduction:** PCA eliminates less significant components, which often correspond to noise, improving the signal-to-noise ratio.
- **Efficiency:** By minimizing the number of dimensions, PCA reduces computational costs and storage requirements.
- **Feature Selection:** PCA highlights the most important features driving variance in the data, aiding in feature engineering.

Limitations of PCA

- **Linear Assumption:** PCA assumes that relationships between features are linear, which may limit its effectiveness for non-linear datasets.
- **Interpretability:** The transformed features (principal components) may not have a clear interpretation, making it harder to explain results.
- **Scaling Dependence:** Proper standardization is crucial, as unscaled features can distort the principal components.

Implementation in Python

The following example demonstrates PCA in Python using Scikit-Learn:

Step 1: Importing Libraries

```
from sklearn.decomposition import PCA
from sklearn.preprocessing import StandardScaler
```

Step 2: Example Dataset

We create a simple dataset to illustrate PCA:

```
# Example data
features = [
    [1.0, 1.0],
    [1.5, 2.0],
    [3.0, 4.0],
    [5.0, 7.0],
    [3.5, 5.0],
    [4.5, 5.0],
    [3.5, 4.5]
```

]

Step 3: Standardization

Standardize the features to ensure equal contribution to the principal components:

```
scaler = StandardScaler()
scaled_features = scaler.fit_transform(features)
```

Step 4: Applying PCA

Reduce the data to two dimensions:

```
pca = PCA(n_components=2)
principal_components = pca.fit_transform(scaled_features)
print(principal_components)
```

Output:

The transformed dataset will have reduced dimensions while retaining the maximum variance:

```
[[-2.505, -0.144],
 [-1.927, -0.265],
 [ 0.046, -0.070],
 [ 2.776,  0.204],
 [ 0.658,  0.034],
 [ 1.558, -0.149],
 [ 0.594,  0.389]]
```

Insights from PCA

1. **Variance Explained:** The proportion of variance retained by each principal component can be

analyzed using the explained_variance_ratio_ attribute in Scikit-Learn:

```
print(pca.explained_variance_ratio_)
```

2. **Dimensionality Reduction:** By focusing on components that capture significant variance, PCA simplifies datasets while retaining essential information.
3. **Applications:** PCA is widely used in image processing, gene expression analysis, and recommendation systems, where high-dimensional data is prevalent.

Advanced Considerations
Hyperparameter Tuning

- **Number of Components:** Choosing the optimal number of components involves balancing variance retention and dimensionality reduction. Plotting a cumulative explained variance graph can help determine the appropriate number:

```
import matplotlib.pyplot as plt
cumulative_variance = pca.explained_variance_ratio_.cumsum()
plt.plot(range(1, len(cumulative_variance)+1), cumulative_variance)
plt.xlabel('Number of Components')
plt.ylabel('Cumulative Explained Variance')
plt.title('Explained Variance vs. Number of Components')
plt.show()
```

Non-Linear Dimensionality Reduction

For datasets with non-linear structures, techniques like Kernel PCA, t-SNE, or UMAP may be more effective. Kernel PCA extends PCA by incorporating kernel functions to capture non-linear relationships.

Combining PCA with Clustering

PCA is often used as a preprocessing step before clustering algorithms like K-Means, enhancing their performance on high-dimensional datasets by reducing noise and computational complexity.

PCA is a fundamental tool for dimensionality reduction, enabling the simplification of complex datasets while preserving their variance. By transforming data into a lower-dimensional space, PCA facilitates visualization, enhances computational efficiency, and improves the interpretability of machine learning models. Despite its limitations, PCA remains a cornerstone technique in data analysis, offering powerful insights and paving the way for more advanced analyses.

Real-World Example: Customer Segmentation Using Python

Customer segmentation is one of the most impactful applications of unsupervised learning in marketing and business analytics. It involves dividing customers into distinct groups based on shared characteristics or behaviors, enabling businesses to tailor their marketing strategies, enhance customer satisfaction, and optimize resource allocation. In this example, we demonstrate how K-Means clustering can be applied to segment customers based on their demographic and behavioral data.

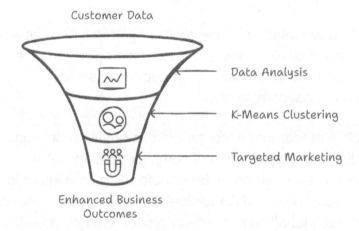

Dataset Description

The dataset used for this example contains three features:

- **Age:** The age of the customer.
- **Annual Income:** The yearly income of the customer in thousands of dollars.
- **Spending Score:** A score assigned to customers based on their spending habits and behavior (ranging from 1 to 100).

Objective

The goal is to identify meaningful customer segments to enable targeted marketing strategies, such as identifying high-spending customers or value-seeking customers.

Implementation in Python

Below is the step-by-step implementation of customer segmentation using K-Means clustering:

Step 1: Importing Libraries
```
import pandas as pd
from sklearn.cluster import KMeans
from sklearn.preprocessing import StandardScaler
import matplotlib.pyplot as plt
```

Step 2: Creating the Dataset
```
# Example dataset
data = {
    'age': [25, 34, 45, 31, 40, 35, 28, 50],
    'annual_income': [15, 18, 20, 22, 24, 25, 30, 35],
    'spending_score': [39, 81, 6, 77, 40, 76, 94, 3]
}

df = pd.DataFrame(data)
```

Step 3: Standardizing the Data

Since K-Means relies on Euclidean distance, it is essential to standardize the features to ensure equal contribution:

```
scaler = StandardScaler()
scaled_data = scaler.fit_transform(df)
```

Step 4: Applying K-Means Clustering

Cluster the data into three groups:

```
kmeans = KMeans(n_clusters=3, random_state=42)
kmeans.fit(scaled_data)

df['cluster'] = kmeans.labels_
```

Step 5: Visualizing the Clusters

```
plt.scatter(df['annual_income'], df['spending_score'], c=df['cluster'], cmap='viridis')
plt.xlabel('Annual Income')
plt.ylabel('Spending Score')
plt.title('Customer Segmentation')
plt.show()
```

Insights

1. **Cluster Interpretation:**
   - Each cluster represents a distinct group of customers, such as high-income low-spenders, low-income high-spenders, or moderate-income moderate-spenders.
2. **Actionable Strategies:**
   - High-income low-spenders can be targeted with premium offers to encourage spending.
   - Low-income high-spenders may value discounts and loyalty programs.
3. **Visual Analysis:**
   - Visualizing clusters helps businesses identify patterns and outliers, making segmentation more intuitive and actionable.

Advanced Considerations

1. **Choosing the Optimal Number of Clusters:** Use the Elbow Method or Silhouette Analysis to determine the best number of clusters.

```
wcss = []
for i in range(1, 11):
    kmeans = KMeans(n_clusters=i, random_state=42)
    kmeans.fit(scaled_data)
    wcss.append(kmeans.inertia_)

plt.plot(range(1, 11), wcss)
plt.title('Elbow Method')
plt.xlabel('Number of Clusters')
plt.ylabel('WCSS')
plt.show()
```

2. **Feature Engineering:** Additional features such as purchase frequency or product preferences can enhance segmentation.
3. **Evaluation Metrics:** Use metrics like Silhouette Score to evaluate the quality of clustering:

```
from sklearn.metrics import silhouette_score
score = silhouette_score(scaled_data, kmeans.labels_)
print("Silhouette Score:", score)
```

Customer segmentation using K-Means clustering empowers businesses to understand their customers better and make data-driven decisions. By leveraging demographic and behavioral data, companies can craft personalized marketing campaigns, improve customer satisfaction, and drive revenue growth. This example illustrates the power of unsupervised learning in uncovering hidden patterns and creating actionable insights in the business world.

6. Deep Learning with Python

Deep learning is a transformative subset of machine learning that emphasizes algorithms modeled after the structure and function of the human brain. These sophisticated algorithms, known as neural networks, are designed to process large amounts of data and extract meaningful patterns, enabling them to perform tasks that were once considered exclusively human. Fields such as computer vision, natural language processing, reinforcement learning, and even generative art have been revolutionized by the advancements in deep learning. The ability of these networks to learn from raw data and make predictions has opened new possibilities across industries, including healthcare, finance, and autonomous systems. This chapter provides a comprehensive introduction to the foundational concepts of deep learning and practical implementations using Python, making it accessible for both beginners and experienced practitioners.

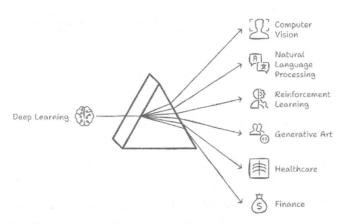

Unveiling the Power of Deep Learning

Introduction to Neural Networks

Neural networks are at the core of deep learning, a subset of machine learning that focuses on algorithms inspired by the structure and functioning of the human brain. These networks consist of layers of interconnected nodes, referred to as neurons, that work collaboratively to analyze data, identify patterns, and make predictions or classifications. The ability of neural networks to process vast amounts of data and uncover intricate relationships makes them a powerful tool for solving complex problems in diverse fields such as healthcare, finance, and artificial intelligence.

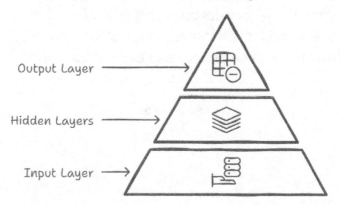

Components of a Neural Network

1. **Input Layer**: The input layer serves as the gateway for raw data to enter the neural network. Each neuron in this layer corresponds to a specific feature of the input data. For example, in an image recognition task,

each neuron might represent a pixel value of an image. This layer prepares the data for further processing by subsequent layers.
2. **Hidden Layers**: Hidden layers are the computational backbone of a neural network. These layers consist of neurons that apply mathematical transformations to the input data. Each neuron computes a weighted sum of its inputs, adds a bias term, and passes the result through an activation function. The number and configuration of hidden layers greatly influence the network's ability to learn complex patterns. Networks with more hidden layers are referred to as deep neural networks.
3. **Output Layer**: The output layer generates the final predictions or classifications of the neural network. The number of neurons in this layer depends on the specific task. For example, in a binary classification task, the output layer typically contains one neuron, while a multi-class classification task requires multiple neurons, each representing a class.

Key Concepts

- **Weights and Biases**: Weights represent the strength of the connection between two neurons, determining how much influence one neuron has on another. Biases are additional parameters that shift the activation function, enabling the network to fit the data more flexibly. Together, weights and biases form the trainable parameters of a neural network.
- **Activation Functions**: Activation functions introduce non-linearity into the network, allowing it to model

complex relationships in the data. Common activation functions include:
  - **ReLU (Rectified Linear Unit)**: Sets all negative values to zero, preserving positive values. It is computationally efficient and widely used.
  - **Sigmoid**: Maps input values to a range between 0 and 1, often used in the output layer for binary classification.
  - **Tanh**: Similar to Sigmoid but maps values to a range between -1 and 1, providing stronger gradients for negative values.
- **Loss Function**: The loss function quantifies the difference between the predicted output and the actual target values. It provides feedback to the network during training, guiding it to adjust its parameters. Examples include Mean Squared Error (MSE) for regression tasks and Cross-Entropy Loss for classification tasks.
- **Backpropagation**: Backpropagation is an optimization technique used to update the weights and biases of a neural network. It involves:

0. Calculating the loss using the loss function.
1. Propagating the error backward through the network.
2. Updating weights and biases using algorithms like gradient descent, which minimizes the loss function by iteratively adjusting the parameters.

Applications of Neural Networks

Neural networks have revolutionized numerous domains by enabling machines to perform tasks once considered exclusive to humans. Some notable applications include:

- **Image Recognition**: Identifying objects, faces, or scenes in images, with applications in security and social media.
- **Natural Language Processing (NLP)**: Understanding and generating human language for chatbots, translation systems, and sentiment analysis.
- **Medical Diagnosis**: Assisting in detecting diseases from medical images like X-rays or MRIs.
- **Financial Forecasting**: Predicting stock prices and assessing credit risk.
- **Autonomous Vehicles**: Enabling self-driving cars to perceive their environment and make decisions.

The Future of Neural Networks

As computational power continues to grow and access to large datasets becomes more prevalent, the capabilities of neural networks are expected to expand further. Innovations such as transfer learning, neural architecture search, and quantum neural networks are paving the way for more efficient and powerful models. Neural networks are poised to play an even more significant role in shaping the future of technology and society.

In summary, neural networks are a transformative technology that mimics the human brain's ability to learn and adapt. By leveraging components such as layers, weights, biases, activation functions, and backpropagation, these networks can tackle some of the most challenging problems in science and industry. With continued advancements, the potential applications and impacts of neural networks are virtually limitless.

Building a Neural Network Using TensorFlow and Keras

TensorFlow and Keras are among the most widely used libraries for developing and training neural networks. TensorFlow is a comprehensive open-source platform for machine learning, while Keras provides a user-friendly, high-level API that simplifies model creation, training, and evaluation.

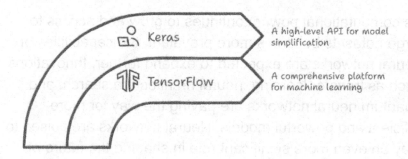

Components of Neural Network Development

Keras — A high-level API for model simplification

TensorFlow — A comprehensive platform for machine learning

Step-by-Step Guide to Building a Neural Network

Step 1: Importing Libraries

To start, import the necessary libraries. TensorFlow provides the core framework, and Keras offers the tools for building neural network layers.

```
import tensorflow as tf
from tensorflow.keras.models import Sequential
from tensorflow.keras.layers import Dense
```

Step 2: Preparing the Dataset

For demonstration purposes, we use a synthetic dataset generated with the make_regression function. The dataset simulates a regression task where the target variable depends on input features.

```
from sklearn.datasets import make_regression
from sklearn.model_selection import train_test_split
from sklearn.preprocessing import StandardScaler

# Create dataset
X, y = make_regression(n_samples=1000, n_features=10, noise=0.1)

# Split data into training and testing sets
X_train, X_test, y_train, y_test = train_test_split(X, y, test_size=0.2, random_state=42)

# Scale data for better performance
scaler = StandardScaler()
X_train = scaler.fit_transform(X_train)
X_test = scaler.transform(X_test)
```

Step 3: Defining the Model

Define a Sequential model with multiple Dense layers. Each Dense layer represents a fully connected layer in the neural network.

```
model = Sequential([
    Dense(64, activation='relu', input_shape=(X_train.shape[1],)),  # First hidden layer
    Dense(32, activation='relu'),                                    # Second hidden layer
    Dense(1)                                                         # Output layer for regression
])
```

- **64, 32, and 1**: These numbers represent the number of neurons in each layer.
- **Activation Functions**: The ReLU activation function introduces non-linearity to help the model learn complex patterns.

Step 4: Compiling the Model

Before training, compile the model by specifying the optimizer, loss function, and metrics to monitor during training.

```
model.compile(optimizer='adam', loss='mse', metrics=['mae'])
```

- **Optimizer**: The Adam optimizer adapts the learning rate and accelerates convergence.
- **Loss Function**: Mean Squared Error (MSE) is commonly used for regression tasks.

- **Metrics**: Mean Absolute Error (MAE) provides additional feedback on model performance.

Step 5: Training the Model

Train the model using the fit method. This method iterates over the dataset for a specified number of epochs.

```
history = model.fit(X_train, y_train, epochs=50, batch_size=32, validation_split=0.2)
```

- **Epochs**: Number of times the model sees the entire training dataset.
- **Batch Size**: Number of samples processed before updating the model parameters.
- **Validation Split**: Percentage of training data reserved for validation.

Step 6: Evaluating the Model

Evaluate the model on the test data to measure its performance.

```
eval_metrics = model.evaluate(X_test, y_test)
print("Loss:", eval_metrics[0])
print("Mean Absolute Error:", eval_metrics[1])
```

- **Loss**: Measures the error in predictions.
- **MAE**: Provides insight into the average magnitude of errors.

Enhancing the Neural Network

Adding Dropout Layers

Dropout layers help prevent overfitting by randomly disabling neurons during training.

```
from tensorflow.keras.layers import Dropout

model = Sequential([
    Dense(64, activation='relu', input_shape=(X_train.shape[1],)),
    Dropout(0.2),
    Dense(32, activation='relu'),
    Dropout(0.2),
    Dense(1)
])
```

Using Early Stopping

Early stopping halts training when the validation loss stops improving, preventing overfitting.

```
from tensorflow.keras.callbacks import EarlyStopping

early_stopping = EarlyStopping(monitor='val_loss', patience=5)

history = model.fit(
    X_train, y_train, epochs=50, batch_size=32, validation_split=0.2, callbacks=[early_stopping]
)
```

Visualizing Training Results

Plot the training and validation loss to observe the model's learning process.

```
import matplotlib.pyplot as plt

plt.plot(history.history['loss'], label='Training Loss')
plt.plot(history.history['val_loss'], label='Validation Loss')
plt.xlabel('Epochs')
plt.ylabel('Loss')
plt.legend()
plt.show()
```

By following this guide, you can build and train a simple neural network using TensorFlow and Keras. This example serves as a foundation for exploring more complex architectures and tasks. Experiment with different configurations, optimizers, and hyperparameters to improve model performance.

Convolutional Neural Networks (CNNs) for Image Classification

Convolutional Neural Networks (CNNs) are a class of deep learning models specifically designed to process and analyze visual data. They are widely used in computer vision tasks such as image classification, object detection, and image segmentation. CNNs utilize specialized layers to extract and learn spatial hierarchies of features from input images, making them particularly effective for handling high-dimensional data like images.

Key Components of CNNs

1. **Convolutional Layers**:
    - These layers apply a set of filters (or kernels) to the input image, producing feature maps.

- Each filter is designed to detect specific patterns, such as edges, textures, or colors.
  - The convolution operation preserves the spatial relationship between pixels by learning image features in small local regions.
  - Example parameters include the number of filters, filter size (e.g., 3x3), stride, and padding.
2. **Pooling Layers**:
    - Pooling layers reduce the spatial dimensions of the feature maps, decreasing the computational requirements and helping to prevent overfitting.
    - Common pooling methods include MaxPooling (selects the maximum value in a region) and AveragePooling (computes the average value).
    - Pooling helps retain the most important features while discarding redundant information.
3. **Fully Connected Layers**:
    - These layers are traditional dense layers that connect every neuron in one layer to every neuron in the next.
    - Fully connected layers aggregate the spatially extracted features from convolutional and pooling layers to make final predictions.
4. **Activation Functions**:
    - Non-linear activation functions such as ReLU (Rectified Linear Unit) introduce non-linearity, enabling the model to learn complex mappings.

- The final layer typically uses a softmax activation function for multi-class classification tasks, producing probabilities for each class.
5. **Dropout Layers** (Optional):
    - Dropout randomly disables a fraction of neurons during training, helping to prevent overfitting and improve generalization.

Implementation Example: Image Classification

The following example demonstrates how to build a simple CNN for classifying images from the CIFAR-10 dataset.

Step 1: Import Libraries
```
from tensorflow.keras.models import Sequential
from tensorflow.keras.layers import Conv2D, MaxPooling2D, Flatten, Dense
from tensorflow.keras.datasets import cifar10
from tensorflow.keras.utils import to_categorical
```

Step 2: Load and Preprocess Data
```
# Load dataset
(X_train, y_train), (X_test, y_test) = cifar10.load_data()

# Normalize pixel values to the range [0, 1]
X_train, X_test = X_train / 255.0, X_test / 255.0

# Convert labels to one-hot encoding
y_train, y_test = to_categorical(y_train), to_categorical(y_test)
```

Step 3: Define the Model
```
model = Sequential([
    Conv2D(32, (3, 3), activation='relu', input_shape=(32, 32, 3)),  # First convolutional layer
    MaxPooling2D((2, 2)),                           # First pooling layer
```

```
    Conv2D(64, (3, 3), activation='relu'),              # Second convolutional layer
    MaxPooling2D((2, 2)),                               # Second pooling layer
    Flatten(),                                          # Flatten the feature maps
    Dense(64, activation='relu'),                       # Fully connected layer
    Dense(10, activation='softmax')                     # Output layer for 10 classes
])
```

Step 4: Compile the Model
```
model.compile(optimizer='adam', loss='categorical_crossentropy', metrics=['accuracy'])
```

- **Optimizer**: The Adam optimizer combines the benefits of AdaGrad and RMSProp, making it highly effective for CNNs.
- **Loss Function**: Categorical crossentropy is used for multi-class classification tasks.
- **Metrics**: Accuracy is a common metric for evaluating classification performance.

Step 5: Train the Model
```
history = model.fit(X_train, y_train, epochs=10, batch_size=64, validation_split=0.2)
```

- **Epochs**: Number of complete passes through the training dataset.
- **Batch Size**: Number of samples processed at a time during training.
- **Validation Split**: Fraction of training data used for validation.

Step 6: Evaluate the Model

```
loss, accuracy = model.evaluate(X_test, y_test)
print("Test Loss:", loss)
print("Test Accuracy:", accuracy)
```

Visualizing Model Performance

Plot the training and validation accuracy and loss over epochs to assess the model's performance.

```
import matplotlib.pyplot as plt

# Plot training and validation accuracy
plt.plot(history.history['accuracy'], label='Training Accuracy')
plt.plot(history.history['val_accuracy'], label='Validation Accuracy')
plt.xlabel('Epochs')
plt.ylabel('Accuracy')
plt.legend()
plt.show()

# Plot training and validation loss
plt.plot(history.history['loss'], label='Training Loss')
plt.plot(history.history['val_loss'], label='Validation Loss')
plt.xlabel('Epochs')
plt.ylabel('Loss')
plt.legend()
plt.show()
```

Enhancements to CNNs

1. **Data Augmentation**:
   - Augmenting the dataset by applying transformations such as rotations, flips, and zooms can increase model robustness.
2. **Transfer Learning**:

- Leveraging pre-trained models such as VGG, ResNet, or Inception as a starting point can accelerate training and improve performance, especially for smaller datasets.
3. **Batch Normalization**:
    - Adding batch normalization layers can stabilize training by normalizing inputs to each layer.
4. **Advanced Architectures**:
    - Explore deeper architectures with additional convolutional and pooling layers for more complex tasks.

CNNs are a powerful tool for image classification and other computer vision tasks. By following this guide, you can build, train, and evaluate a simple CNN using TensorFlow and Keras. With practice and experimentation, you can extend this basic model to tackle more challenging image recognition problems.

Real-World Example: Handwritten Digit Recognition (MNIST Dataset)

The MNIST dataset is one of the most well-known benchmarks in the field of deep learning and computer vision. It contains 70,000 grayscale images of handwritten digits, each representing a digit from 0 to 9. The dataset is widely used for demonstrating the power of neural networks, particularly convolutional neural networks (CNNs), in solving image classification tasks.

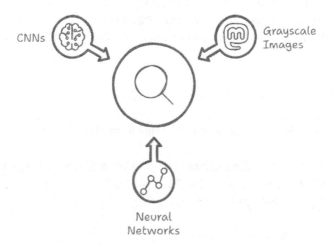

Characteristics of the MNIST Dataset

- **Image Size**: Each image is 28x28 pixels.
- **Grayscale Values**: Pixel values range from 0 to 255, where 0 represents black and 255 represents white.
- **Classes**: There are 10 classes (digits 0 through 9).
- **Training Set**: 60,000 images.
- **Test Set**: 10,000 images.

Objective

The goal is to classify each image into one of the 10 digit classes using a convolutional neural network (CNN).

Implementation

Below is a step-by-step implementation using TensorFlow and Keras.

Step 1: Import Libraries
```
from tensorflow.keras.datasets import mnist
from tensorflow.keras.utils import to_categorical
from tensorflow.keras.models import Sequential
from tensorflow.keras.layers import Conv2D, MaxPooling2D, Flatten, Dense
```

Step 2: Load and Preprocess the Data
```
# Load dataset
(X_train, y_train), (X_test, y_test) = mnist.load_data()

# Reshape data to include channel dimension and normalize pixel values
X_train = X_train.reshape(-1, 28, 28, 1) / 255.0
X_test = X_test.reshape(-1, 28, 28, 1) / 255.0

# Convert labels to one-hot encoding
y_train, y_test = to_categorical(y_train), to_categorical(y_test)
```

Step 3: Define the Model
```
model = Sequential([
    Conv2D(32, (3, 3), activation='relu', input_shape=(28, 28, 1)),  # First convolutional layer
    MaxPooling2D((2, 2)),                       # First pooling layer
    Flatten(),                                  # Flatten feature maps
    Dense(64, activation='relu'),               # Fully connected layer
    Dense(10, activation='softmax')             # Output layer for 10 classes
])
```

Step 4: Compile the Model
```
model.compile(optimizer='adam', loss='categorical_crossentropy', metrics=['accuracy'])
```

- **Optimizer**: Adam is a versatile optimizer combining the benefits of AdaGrad and RMSProp.

- **Loss Function**: Categorical Crossentropy is used for multi-class classification.
- **Metrics**: Accuracy is the performance metric.

Step 5: Train the Model

```
history = model.fit(X_train, y_train, epochs=10, batch_size=64, validation_split=0.2)
```

- **Epochs**: Specifies the number of complete passes through the dataset.
- **Batch Size**: Defines the number of samples processed before updating the model.
- **Validation Split**: Reserves 20% of the training data for validation.

Step 6: Evaluate the Model

```
loss, accuracy = model.evaluate(X_test, y_test)
print("Test Loss:", loss)
print("Test Accuracy:", accuracy)
```

Insights from the MNIST Example

1. **Effectiveness of CNNs**:
   - CNNs are particularly well-suited for image classification tasks due to their ability to learn spatial hierarchies of features (e.g., edges, textures, and shapes).
2. **Simplicity of Architecture**:
   - Even with a relatively simple architecture, it is possible to achieve high accuracy on the MNIST dataset. This demonstrates the potential of deep learning for solving practical problems.

3. **Generalization**:
    - Training on 60,000 images and achieving high accuracy on the separate test set of 10,000 images showcases the model's ability to generalize to unseen data.
4. **Preprocessing**:
    - Normalization of pixel values and one-hot encoding of labels are essential preprocessing steps that significantly improve model performance.

Enhancements for Better Performance

1. **Data Augmentation**:
    - Generate additional training data by applying transformations such as rotations, shifts, and zooms.
2. **Deeper Architectures**:
    - Add more convolutional and pooling layers to improve the model's feature extraction capabilities.
3. **Dropout Layers**:
    - Introduce dropout layers to reduce overfitting and improve generalization.
4. **Learning Rate Scheduling**:
    - Use a learning rate scheduler to dynamically adjust the learning rate during training.
5. **Transfer Learning**:
    - Use pre-trained models on similar datasets to accelerate training and potentially improve accuracy.

The MNIST dataset serves as a gateway to understanding and applying deep learning for image classification. By leveraging CNNs and frameworks like TensorFlow and Keras, we can build powerful models capable of solving real-world problems. The principles demonstrated in this example can be extended to more complex datasets and tasks, paving the way for advancements in artificial intelligence and machine learning.

7. Natural Language Processing with Python

Natural Language Processing (NLP) is a dynamic and rapidly evolving subfield of artificial intelligence that focuses on enabling machines to understand, interpret, and respond to human language in both written and spoken forms. It bridges the gap between human communication and machine comprehension, making it possible for computers to process, analyze, and even generate natural language text and speech. Python, with its vast ecosystem of powerful libraries and frameworks, has emerged as the preferred language for tackling NLP tasks. Its versatility and the availability of robust libraries like NLTK, spaCy, and others allow developers to seamlessly implement a wide range of NLP applications, from sentiment analysis to chatbots. This chapter delves into the foundational concepts of NLP, shedding light on its significance, and presents practical, hands-on examples using popular Python libraries such as NLTK and spaCy.

Text Preprocessing with NLTK and spaCy

Text preprocessing is a foundational step in the Natural Language Processing (NLP) pipeline. It is crucial for converting unstructured raw text into a structured format that is easier to analyze. This process often includes tasks like tokenization, stopword removal, stemming, lemmatization, and more. Two widely used Python libraries for text preprocessing are **NLTK (Natural Language Toolkit)** and

spaCy. Each offers unique features and capabilities suited to various NLP tasks.

NLTK

NLTK is a comprehensive and highly flexible library for text processing. It provides tools for tokenization, stemming, lemmatization, and stopword removal, along with other functionalities for text analysis. NLTK is particularly suited for academic research and experimentation due to its flexibility and the wide range of datasets it offers. It also includes a host of linguistic resources like WordNet, which is invaluable for tasks such as synonym generation, antonym detection, and hypernym analysis.

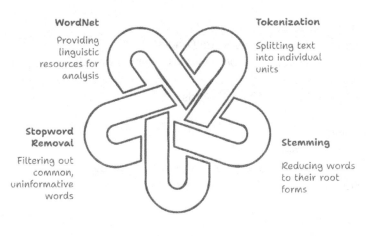

NLTK's Text Processing Capabilities

WordNet — Providing linguistic resources for analysis

Tokenization — Splitting text into individual units

Stopword Removal — Filtering out common, uninformative words

Stemming — Reducing words to their root forms

Lemmatization — Converting words to their base forms

Example: Basic Text Preprocessing with NLTK

```python
import nltk
from nltk.tokenize import word_tokenize, sent_tokenize
from nltk.corpus import stopwords
from nltk.stem import PorterStemmer
from nltk.stem import WordNetLemmatizer

# Download necessary NLTK data files
nltk.download('punkt')
nltk.download('stopwords')
nltk.download('wordnet')

text = "Natural Language Processing enables machines to understand human language."

# Tokenization
word_tokens = word_tokenize(text)
sent_tokens = sent_tokenize(text)
print("Word Tokens:", word_tokens)
print("Sentence Tokens:", sent_tokens)

# Remove stopwords
stop_words = set(stopwords.words('english'))
filtered_words = [word for word in word_tokens if word.lower() not in stop_words]
print("Filtered Words:", filtered_words)

# Stemming
ps = PorterStemmer()
stemmed_words = [ps.stem(word) for word in filtered_words]
print("Stemmed Words:", stemmed_words)

# Lemmatization
lemmatizer = WordNetLemmatizer()
lemmatized_words = [lemmatizer.lemmatize(word) for word in filtered_words]
print("Lemmatized Words:", lemmatized_words)
```

Key Features of NLTK:

1. **Tokenization**: Splits text into words and sentences, enabling finer granularity for analysis.
2. **Stopword Removal**: Filters out common words like "the," "is," "in," etc., that do not add significant value to the context.
3. **Stemming**: Reduces words to their root forms (e.g., "running" to "run"), simplifying text while retaining its meaning.
4. **Lemmatization**: Converts words to their base forms (e.g., "better" to "good"), offering a more linguistically accurate representation compared to stemming.
5. **Extensive Datasets**: Includes corpora like WordNet and tools for linguistic analysis, making it a go-to library for educational and research purposes.

spaCy

spaCy is a fast, production-ready NLP library designed for efficient processing of large text datasets. It is particularly strong in tasks such as named entity recognition (NER), dependency parsing, and part-of-speech tagging. Unlike NLTK, spaCy focuses on modern NLP workflows, emphasizing performance and scalability. This makes it a preferred choice for developers and data scientists working on industrial applications or real-time systems.

Example: Text Processing with spaCy
```
import spacy

# Load spaCy model
nlp = spacy.load("en_core_web_sm")
```

```python
text = "Natural Language Processing enables machines to understand human language."

doc = nlp(text)

# Tokenization
print("Tokens:", [token.text for token in doc])

# Part-of-Speech Tagging
print("POS Tags:", [(token.text, token.pos_) for token in doc])

# Named Entity Recognition
print("Entities:", [(ent.text, ent.label_) for ent in doc.ents])
```

Key Features of spaCy:

1. **Efficient Tokenization**: Processes text quickly and accurately, handling edge cases seamlessly.
2. **Part-of-Speech (POS) Tagging**: Assigns grammatical tags to words, aiding syntactic analysis.
3. **Named Entity Recognition (NER)**: Identifies entities such as names, dates, and organizations, which is crucial for information extraction tasks.
4. **Dependency Parsing**: Analyzes grammatical structure to understand relationships between words.
5. **Pre-trained Models**: Includes models for multiple languages with support for deep learning integration, enabling tasks like sentiment analysis and classification.

Comparison: NLTK vs. spaCy

Feature	NLTK	spaCy
Ease of Use	Flexible but requires manual setup	Easy to use with pre-built models
Performance	Slower due to flexibility	Optimized for speed and efficiency
Applications	Academic and experimental research	Production and large-scale systems
Features	Comprehensive with corpora	Focused on modern NLP tasks
Community Support	Extensive with many resources	Growing, with focus on industry use

Advanced Techniques with NLTK and spaCy

NLTK:

- **Synonym Replacement**: Using WordNet to find synonyms for words, enhancing text variability.
- **Text Classification**: Building machine learning models for tasks like sentiment analysis, spam detection, and text categorization.
- **Contextual Parsing**: Creating custom parsers for domain-specific tasks, such as medical or legal text analysis.

spaCy:

- **Custom Pipelines**: Adding custom components to processing pipelines to tailor spaCy to specific project needs.
- **Word Vector Similarity**: Using pre-trained word embeddings for semantic analysis, enabling nuanced understanding of text.
- **Integration with Deep Learning**: Works seamlessly with libraries like TensorFlow and PyTorch, allowing the integration of advanced neural models for NLP tasks.

When to Use NLTK or spaCy

- **NLTK**: Ideal for beginners, research projects, or tasks requiring extensive customization and access to linguistic datasets.
- **spaCy**: Best for production environments, large-scale text processing tasks, and applications requiring speed and efficiency.

By understanding the strengths and use cases of both libraries, you can select the best tool for your NLP project and achieve optimal results. Whether you are conducting exploratory research or deploying a real-time application, leveraging the right library is essential for success in the field of Natural Language Processing.

Building a Sentiment Analysis Model in Python

Sentiment analysis, often referred to as opinion mining, is a key application of Natural Language Processing (NLP). It involves identifying and categorizing the sentiment expressed in text, such as positive, negative, or neutral. Sentiment analysis has widespread use cases, including social media monitoring, customer feedback analysis, and brand reputation management. Python's versatile libraries like **TextBlob** and **scikit-learn** make building sentiment analysis models straightforward and effective.

Sentiment Analysis with TextBlob

TextBlob is a simple yet powerful library built on top of NLTK and provides an easy-to-use interface for common NLP tasks, including sentiment analysis.

Example: Sentiment Analysis with TextBlob

```
from textblob import TextBlob

text = "I love natural language processing! It's so fascinating."
blob = TextBlob(text)

# Sentiment Analysis
sentiment = blob.sentiment
print("Polarity:", sentiment.polarity)  # Range from -1 (negative) to 1 (positive)
print("Subjectivity:", sentiment.subjectivity)  # Range from 0 (objective) to 1 (subjective)
```

Key Features of TextBlob:

1. **Polarity Scoring**: Measures how positive or negative a sentence is.

2. **Subjectivity Analysis**: Determines whether text is factual or opinionated.
3. **Ease of Use**: Minimal setup and user-friendly syntax make it ideal for quick implementations.

The TextBlob library is perfect for beginners looking to quickly dive into sentiment analysis without extensive configuration.

Sentiment Analysis with scikit-learn

scikit-learn is a robust library for machine learning in Python. It allows for creating custom sentiment analysis models by leveraging algorithms like Naïve Bayes, Support Vector Machines, and Random Forests.

Example: Sentiment Analysis with scikit-learn

```
from sklearn.feature_extraction.text import CountVectorizer
from sklearn.model_selection import train_test_split
from sklearn.naive_bayes import MultinomialNB

# Sample dataset
texts = [
    "I love this product!",
    "This is the worst experience I've ever had.",
    "Amazing quality and fast delivery.",
    "I'm disappointed with the service.",
    "Totally worth the price!"
]
labels = [1, 0, 1, 0, 1]  # 1 for positive, 0 for negative

# Vectorize text data
vectorizer = CountVectorizer()
X = vectorizer.fit_transform(texts)

# Split data
```

```python
X_train, X_test, y_train, y_test = train_test_split(X, labels, test_size=0.2, random_state=42)

# Train model
model = MultinomialNB()
model.fit(X_train, y_train)

# Evaluate model
accuracy = model.score(X_test, y_test)
print("Accuracy:", accuracy)
```

Key Features of scikit-learn:

1. **Customizability**: Build sentiment analysis models tailored to specific datasets.
2. **Machine Learning Algorithms**: Leverage powerful classifiers like Naïve Bayes, SVMs, and logistic regression.
3. **Extensive Feature Engineering**: Incorporates tools for text vectorization, such as CountVectorizer and TfidfVectorizer.

Comparison: TextBlob vs. scikit-learn

Feature	TextBlob	scikit-learn
Ease of Use	User-friendly, minimal configuration	Requires understanding of ML concepts
Performance	Suitable for small datasets	Handles larger datasets effectively
Applications	Quick sentiment scoring	Customizable models for specific needs
Flexibility	Limited	Highly flexible and extendable

Applications of Sentiment Analysis

1. **Social Media Monitoring**: Analyze public opinion about brands, products, or events on platforms like Twitter and Facebook.
2. **Customer Feedback**: Extract insights from product reviews, service ratings, and customer comments.
3. **Market Research**: Gauge market trends and consumer sentiment to inform business strategies.
4. **Healthcare**: Understand patient sentiment from feedback forms or online reviews.
5. **Political Analysis**: Analyze sentiment around political campaigns, speeches, and policies.

Advanced Techniques in Sentiment Analysis

Ensemble Methods:

Combining multiple algorithms to improve prediction accuracy, such as using Naïve Bayes and Random Forests together.

Pre-trained Models:

Leveraging pre-trained deep learning models like BERT and GPT for contextual sentiment analysis.

Feature Engineering:

Using techniques like TF-IDF, n-grams, and word embeddings to enhance the representation of textual data.

Sentiment analysis is a powerful tool for extracting actionable insights from textual data. Whether you are building a simple model using TextBlob or crafting a robust solution with scikit-learn, Python's ecosystem provides all the necessary tools to get started. By understanding the strengths and limitations of each approach, you can tailor your sentiment analysis pipeline to meet specific project requirements.

Real-World Example: Creating a Python-Based Chatbot

Building a chatbot is an excellent way to combine several Natural Language Processing (NLP) techniques, including text preprocessing, intent classification, and response generation. Chatbots are increasingly used in industries like e-commerce, customer support, education, and healthcare to automate interactions and provide users with instant assistance. Python offers a versatile and robust environment for creating chatbots, with libraries and frameworks like **ChatterBot**, **NLTK**, and **spaCy** simplifying the process.

Example: Simple Chatbot with ChatterBot

ChatterBot is a Python library designed to create conversational chatbots with minimal effort. It comes with pre-built training data and supports multilingual responses, making it a great starting point for beginners.

Implementation
```
from chatterbot import ChatBot
from chatterbot.trainers import ChatterBotCorpusTrainer
```

```
# Create chatbot
chatbot = ChatBot('NLPBot')

# Train chatbot on English corpus
data_path = "chatterbot.corpus.english"
trainer = ChatterBotCorpusTrainer(chatbot)
trainer.train(data_path)

# Chat with the bot
while True:
    user_input = input("You: ")
    if user_input.lower() == "exit":
        break
    response = chatbot.get_response(user_input)
    print("NLPBot:", response)
```

Key Components of the Chatbot

1. **Text Preprocessing**:
   - Cleaning the input data by removing noise, handling spelling errors, and normalizing text.
   - Tokenizing and vectorizing user inputs for the chatbot to understand them better.
2. **Training Data**:
   - The ChatterBot library uses pre-built corpora for training. Developers can also provide custom data to enhance the bot's accuracy for specific use cases.
3. **Response Generation**:
   - Responses are generated using machine learning algorithms and based on the training data. The chatbot improves over time as it interacts with users.

Customizing Chatbots for Specific Applications

1. Customer Support Chatbots

- Use case: Automating responses to common customer inquiries.
- Approach: Integrate FAQs and customer service scripts into the training dataset to provide accurate and context-aware responses.

2. E-commerce Chatbots

- Use case: Assisting customers with product recommendations, order tracking, and payment queries.
- Approach: Combine the chatbot with product catalogs and user behavior analysis to offer personalized interactions.

3. Healthcare Chatbots

- Use case: Providing medical advice, scheduling appointments, and answering health-related questions.
- Approach: Train the chatbot using verified medical guidelines to ensure accurate and safe interactions.

Advantages of Using Python for Chatbots

1. **Ease of Use**: Python's simple syntax and extensive library support make it an ideal choice for developing chatbots.

2. **Flexibility**: Python allows for integration with various APIs, databases, and web frameworks, enabling dynamic chatbot functionality.
3. **Scalability**: Libraries like TensorFlow and PyTorch can be incorporated into chatbot designs to support advanced features such as deep learning-based intent recognition.
4. **Community Support**: Python boasts a large developer community, providing a wealth of tutorials, documentation, and troubleshooting resources.

Insights and Applications

1. **Text Preprocessing**:
   - Cleaning and structuring text data is a fundamental step for achieving high accuracy in NLP tasks, including chatbot development.
2. **Sentiment Analysis**:
   - Incorporate sentiment analysis to detect user emotions and tailor responses accordingly. For example, understanding whether a customer is frustrated or satisfied can improve engagement.
3. **Personalization**:
   - Enhance user experiences by integrating chatbots with user profiles, preferences, and history for more relevant interactions.
4. **Automation**:
   - Automate routine tasks such as customer inquiries, appointment scheduling, or product recommendations, freeing up human resources for complex issues.

By mastering Python's NLP libraries and tools, developers can unlock powerful capabilities to analyze and interpret human language. These advancements drive innovation in artificial intelligence, machine learning, and conversational systems. Whether you're building a simple FAQ bot or a complex AI assistant, Python equips you with the tools to bring your chatbot ideas to life.

8. Reinforcement Learning in Python

Reinforcement Learning (RL) represents a fascinating and dynamic area of machine learning, where agents learn to make decisions by continuously interacting with their environment. Unlike supervised learning, which relies on labeled datasets to guide the model, RL agents operate in an exploratory framework, relying on trial and error to adapt and improve their strategies. This adaptive learning process is driven by a reward system, where positive reinforcement encourages desired actions, and negative feedback discourages suboptimal choices. The versatility of RL has made it instrumental in addressing complex challenges, including mastering games like Go and Chess, optimizing robotic movements, managing dynamic resource allocation, and enabling autonomous navigation. By learning from direct interaction rather than pre-annotated data, RL embodies a core principle of intelligent systems: adapting to uncertainty and evolving through experience.

Fundamentals of Reinforcement Learning

Reinforcement Learning (RL) is a compelling and foundational paradigm in artificial intelligence that focuses on decision-making through interaction with an environment. Unlike supervised learning, where models learn from labeled examples, RL relies on trial-and-error learning to maximize rewards over time. This approach is modeled after the way humans and animals learn from their experiences, making it an intuitive and powerful framework for solving sequential decision-making problems.

Key Components of Reinforcement Learning

RL systems are built on three core components:

1. **Agent**:
   - The decision-maker in the RL system. The agent observes the state of the environment and selects actions based on a policy. Examples include a robot navigating a maze or an AI player in a video game.
2. **Environment**:
   - The external system the agent interacts with. It provides feedback in the form of rewards and changes its state in response to the agent's actions. Environments can be simulated (like a game) or real-world (like a robotic arm).
3. **Reward Signal**:
   - A scalar value that guides the agent's learning process. Positive rewards encourage desirable behavior, while negative rewards discourage undesirable actions. For instance, a robot successfully reaching its target might receive a positive reward, while colliding with obstacles results in a penalty.

The overarching goal of the agent is to learn an **optimal policy** that maximizes the cumulative reward over time. Achieving this requires balancing exploration (trying new actions to discover rewards) and exploitation (choosing actions known to yield high rewards).

Essential Concepts in Reinforcement Learning

1. **State**:
    - Represents the current situation or configuration of the environment. It provides the agent with all the necessary information to make decisions. For example, in a chess game, the state includes the positions of all the pieces on the board.
2. **Action**:
    - The set of possible moves the agent can take in a given state. For example, a robot might move forward, backward, or rotate.
3. **Policy (π)**:
    - A strategy or mapping that defines the agent's actions based on the current state. Policies can be deterministic (always selecting the same action for a state) or stochastic (selecting actions probabilistically).
4. **Value Function (V)**:
    - Measures the long-term expected reward for being in a specific state and following a particular policy. The value function helps the agent evaluate the desirability of states.
5. **Q-Value (Q)**:
    - Extends the value function by incorporating actions. It represents the expected reward for taking a specific action in a specific state and then following the policy. This is central to algorithms like Q-Learning.

Mathematical Framework of RL

Reinforcement Learning is often formulated as a Markov Decision Process (MDP), defined by:

- **States (S)**: A set of all possible configurations of the environment.
- **Actions (A)**: A set of all possible actions the agent can take.
- **Transition Probability (P)**: The probability of moving to a new state given the current state and action.
- **Reward Function (R)**: The immediate reward received after transitioning to a new state.
- **Discount Factor (γ)**: A factor between 0 and 1 that balances immediate rewards and future rewards.

The agent's goal in an MDP is to maximize the **cumulative discounted reward**:

$$G_t = R_{t+1} + \gamma R_{t+2} + \gamma^2 R_{t+3} + \dots = \sum_{k=0}^{\infty} \gamma^k R_{t+k+1}$$

Types of Reinforcement Learning Algorithms

1. **Value-Based Methods**:
    - Focus on estimating value functions, such as Q-Learning and SARSA.
    - These methods learn the optimal policy indirectly by maximizing value functions.
2. **Policy-Based Methods**:

        - Learn the policy directly without requiring value functions.
        - Examples include Policy Gradient methods, which optimize policies through gradient ascent.
    3. **Model-Based Methods**:
        - Build a model of the environment's dynamics and use it to plan actions. These methods can be computationally intensive but offer efficiency in certain tasks.

Applications of Reinforcement Learning

Reinforcement Learning has a wide range of real-world applications, including:

1. **Game Playing**:
    - RL has achieved superhuman performance in games like Chess, Go, and StarCraft.
2. **Robotics**:
    - Teaching robots to walk, grasp objects, or navigate obstacles.
3. **Healthcare**:
    - Optimizing treatment plans and resource allocation in hospitals.
4. **Finance**:
    - Developing trading strategies and portfolio optimization.
5. **Autonomous Vehicles**:
    - Enabling self-driving cars to make real-time decisions in complex traffic scenarios.

By mastering these concepts and applying the mathematical tools of RL, developers and researchers can create intelligent systems capable of solving complex problems in dynamic environments.

Implementing Q-Learning in Python

Q-Learning is one of the most popular and widely used reinforcement learning algorithms. It employs a value-based approach to enable an agent to learn the optimal policy by iteratively improving the estimated Q-values. These Q-values, or action-value functions, represent the expected cumulative reward for taking a specific action in a given state and then following the optimal policy thereafter.

The algorithm updates Q-values using the Bellman equation:

$$Q(s,a) \leftarrow Q(s,a) + \alpha [R + \gamma \max_{a'} Q(s',a') - Q(s,a)]$$

Where:

- $Q(s,a)$: Current Q-value for state s and action a.
- α: Learning rate (controls the step size of updates).
- γ: Discount factor (balances immediate and future rewards).
- R: Reward received after taking action a in state s.

- $\max_{a'} Q(s', a')$: Maximum Q-value for the next state s's'.

This iterative update helps the agent converge to an optimal policy over time by balancing exploration and exploitation.

Example: Q-Learning for a Grid World

Below is a Python implementation of Q-Learning applied to a simple grid world environment:

```python
import numpy as np

# Define the environment
states = [0, 1, 2, 3]
actions = ["left", "right"]
rewards = [0, 0, 0, 1]
transitions = {
    0: {"left": 0, "right": 1},
    1: {"left": 0, "right": 2},
    2: {"left": 1, "right": 3},
    3: {"left": 2, "right": 3},
}

# Parameters
gamma = 0.9  # Discount factor
alpha = 0.1  # Learning rate
q_table = np.zeros((len(states), len(actions)))  # Q-Table initialization

# Training loop
for episode in range(1000):
    state = 0  # Start state
    while state != 3:  # Terminal state
        action_idx = np.random.choice(len(actions))
        action = actions[action_idx]
        next_state = transitions[state][action]
```

```
    reward = rewards[next_state]

    # Update Q-value using Bellman equation
    best_next_q = np.max(q_table[next_state])
    q_table[state, action_idx] += alpha * (reward + gamma * best_next_q - q_table[state, action_idx])

    state = next_state  # Transition to the next state

# Display Q-Table
print("Trained Q-Table:")
print(q_table)
```

Understanding the Example

1. **State and Action Representation**:
   - States are represented as integers (e.g., 0,1,2,30, 1, 2, 3).
   - Actions include "left" and "right," corresponding to index positions in the Q-Table.
2. **Rewards and Transitions**:
   - Each state-action pair transitions to a new state defined in the transitions dictionary.
   - The terminal state (state 33) offers the highest reward (11).
3. **Q-Table Initialization**:
   - The Q-Table is initialized with zeros, where rows represent states and columns represent actions.
4. **Training Loop**:
   - The agent explores actions randomly and updates the Q-Table based on the observed rewards and future Q-values.

- Over multiple episodes, the Q-Table converges to an optimal policy.
5. **Policy Extraction**:
    - Once training is complete, the agent can determine the best action for each state by selecting the action with the highest Q-value.

Applications of Q-Learning

1. **Pathfinding and Navigation**:
    - Robots or autonomous agents can learn to navigate mazes or avoid obstacles efficiently.
2. **Game AI**:
    - Q-Learning has been applied to simple games like Tic-Tac-Toe and advanced games such as Atari classics.
3. **Resource Optimization**:
    - Allocate resources dynamically in systems like cloud computing or network routing.
4. **Dynamic Pricing**:
    - Optimize pricing strategies in e-commerce or retail environments.

Advantages of Q-Learning

- **Model-Free**: Does not require knowledge of the environment's dynamics.
- **Generalizable**: Can be applied to various domains with discrete states and actions.
- **Asynchronous Updates**: Learns effectively without needing all states and actions to be visited in every iteration.

Limitations of Q-Learning

- **Scalability**: Struggles with large state or action spaces due to the size of the Q-Table.
- **Exploration vs. Exploitation**: Balancing exploration of new actions and exploitation of known rewards can be challenging.
- **Requires Discrete Spaces**: Traditional Q-Learning is not suited for continuous state or action spaces.

Q-Learning forms the foundation of many advanced reinforcement learning algorithms. By understanding its mechanics and practical applications, developers can design intelligent agents capable of learning and adapting to diverse environments.

Real-World Example: Building an AI for a Simple Game

Reinforcement Learning (RL) is a powerful paradigm that finds significant applications in gaming. By allowing agents to learn optimal strategies through repeated interactions with the game environment, RL opens up possibilities for creating intelligent game-playing systems. One of the simplest yet effective examples of RL in action is building an AI for Tic-Tac-Toe. This classic game offers a manageable environment for demonstrating the principles of state representation, action selection, and reward-based learning.

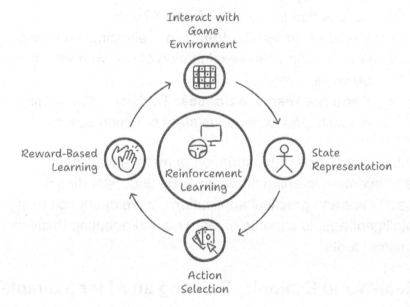

Example: AI for Tic-Tac-Toe

Below is a basic implementation of a Tic-Tac-Toe AI using Python. This example demonstrates the core mechanics of building an AI agent that can learn and play the game effectively.

import random

# Initialize the board
board = [" "] * 9

def print_board():
    for i in range(0, 9, 3):
        print(board[i:i+3])

```python
def check_winner(board):
    winning_combinations = [
        (0, 1, 2), (3, 4, 5), (6, 7, 8),
        (0, 3, 6), (1, 4, 7), (2, 5, 8),
        (0, 4, 8), (2, 4, 6)
    ]
    for x, y, z in winning_combinations:
        if board[x] == board[y] == board[z] and board[x] != " ":
            return board[x]
    return None

def is_draw(board):
    return " " not in board and check_winner(board) is None

# Q-Table for states and actions
q_table = {}

# Function to convert board to a string for Q-Table keys
def board_to_string(board):
    return "".join(board)

# Training the AI
learning_rate = 0.1
reward_win = 1
reward_loss = -1
reward_draw = 0.5
gamma = 0.9

for episode in range(10000):
    board = [" "] * 9
    state = board_to_string(board)
    while " " in board:
        # AI chooses action
        if state not in q_table:
            q_table[state] = [0] * 9  # Initialize Q-values for all actions in this state
        available_moves = [i for i, v in enumerate(board) if v == " "]
```

```python
        move = random.choice(available_moves)
        board[move] = "X"
        next_state = board_to_string(board)

        # Check for winner or opponent's turn
        winner = check_winner(board)
        if winner == "X":
            q_table[state][move] += learning_rate * (reward_win - q_table[state][move])
            break
        elif is_draw(board):
            q_table[state][move] += learning_rate * (reward_draw - q_table[state][move])
            break

        # Opponent plays randomly
        opponent_move = random.choice([i for i, v in enumerate(board) if v == " "])
        board[opponent_move] = "O"
        winner = check_winner(board)

        if winner == "O":
            q_table[state][move] += learning_rate * (reward_loss - q_table[state][move])
            break
        elif is_draw(board):
            q_table[state][move] += learning_rate * (reward_draw - q_table[state][move])
            break

        # Update Q-value
        next_state = board_to_string(board)
        if next_state not in q_table:
            q_table[next_state] = [0] * 9
        q_table[state][move] += learning_rate * (
            gamma * max(q_table[next_state]) - q_table[state][move]
        )
```

```
        state = next_state

# Display trained Q-Table for the initial state
print("Trained Q-Table for the initial state:")
print(q_table[board_to_string([" "] * 9)])
```

Understanding the Example

1. **State Representation**:
    - The board is represented as a list of nine elements. Empty spaces are denoted by " ", and moves by "X" or "O".
    - The state is converted into a string to use as a key in the Q-Table.
2. **Action Selection**:
    - The AI selects actions (moves) randomly during training to explore different strategies.
    - Q-values guide the agent to prefer moves leading to higher rewards in future games.
3. **Rewards**:
    - Winning provides a positive reward, while losing incurs a penalty.
    - Draws are given a neutral reward to encourage learning toward winning.
4. **Learning Dynamics**:
    - The Q-values are updated iteratively using the Bellman equation, balancing immediate and future rewards.

Applications of Game AI

1. **Learning Optimal Strategies**:

- Reinforcement Learning enables agents to identify optimal strategies by playing multiple iterations of the game.
2. **Player Engagement**:
    - AI opponents can provide challenging gameplay experiences for human players.
3. **Testing Game Design**:
    - Game developers can use RL agents to test the balance and fairness of game mechanics.
4. **Teaching and Education**:
    - Simple games like Tic-Tac-Toe can introduce students to RL concepts and algorithms.

Advantages of Reinforcement Learning in Gaming

- Encourages adaptive and intelligent decision-making.
- Does not require labeled data, allowing agents to learn directly from interactions.
- Scalable to more complex games with minor modifications.

By understanding and applying these principles, developers can create game-playing agents that learn and improve over time, showcasing the potential of reinforcement learning in AI-driven solutions.

9. Deploying AI Models with Python

Developing an AI model is only part of the journey; deploying it for real-world use is where its true potential is realized. Deployment transforms static, standalone models into dynamic, accessible tools that can be seamlessly integrated into applications, enabling users to interact with them in meaningful and impactful ways. Python, a versatile and widely-adopted programming language, offers an extensive array of frameworks and libraries, such as Flask and Streamlit, to facilitate the deployment process efficiently and effectively. These tools not only simplify the complexities of deployment but also empower developers to create scalable, robust, and user-friendly solutions that bring AI to life.

The deployment phase involves various key tasks, including exporting and saving models, creating APIs for seamless communication, and designing interactive interfaces for end-users. Each step requires careful planning and execution to ensure the AI model performs reliably in a production environment. By leveraging Python's ecosystem, developers can bridge the gap between the intricate processes of model training and practical usability, delivering solutions that are both innovative and accessible to a broader audience.

Exporting and Saving Models

Exporting and saving AI models is a crucial step in the machine learning pipeline, enabling developers to reuse trained models without the need for retraining. This process is essential for efficient deployment, scalability, and version control of machine learning applications. Python's machine learning libraries, such as scikit-learn, TensorFlow, and PyTorch, offer robust and user-friendly methods for saving and exporting models to various formats.

Why Save Models?

- **Reusability**: Saves time by avoiding the need to retrain the model every time it is used.
- **Portability**: Models can be transferred and used across different environments or platforms.
- **Version Control**: Maintains a snapshot of the model at a particular training stage, allowing comparisons and rollbacks.

Common Formats for Saving Models

- **Pickle (.pkl)**: Common for Python objects, especially in scikit-learn.
- **HDF5 (.h5)**: Used by TensorFlow for saving entire models.
- **ONNX**: A universal format for model exchange between frameworks like PyTorch and TensorFlow.

Saving Models with scikit-learn

scikit-learn provides a simple and efficient way to save models using the joblib library. Here's how to create, save, and load a model:

```
from sklearn.linear_model import LinearRegression
from sklearn.datasets import make_regression
import joblib

# Create and train the model
X, y = make_regression(n_samples=100, n_features=1, noise=0.1)
model = LinearRegression()
model.fit(X, y)

# Save the model
joblib.dump(model, 'linear_regression_model.pkl')

# Load the model
loaded_model = joblib.load('linear_regression_model.pkl')
print("Loaded model prediction:", loaded_model.predict([[2.0]]))
```

This approach ensures your scikit-learn models are easily saved and reloaded for future use.

Saving Models with TensorFlow

TensorFlow simplifies the process of saving and exporting deep learning models. It supports saving either the entire model or just the architecture and weights separately. Below is an example:

```python
import tensorflow as tf
from tensorflow.keras.models import Sequential
from tensorflow.keras.layers import Dense

# Define and train the model
model = Sequential([
    Dense(10, activation='relu'),
    Dense(1)
])
model.compile(optimizer='adam', loss='mse')
model.fit([[1], [2], [3]], [[2], [4], [6]], epochs=100, verbose=0)

# Save the model
model.save('my_model')

# Load the model
loaded_model = tf.keras.models.load_model('my_model')
print("Loaded model prediction:", loaded_model.predict([[4]]))
```

TensorFlow's .save and .load_model methods ensure comprehensive model preservation, including architecture, optimizer configuration, and weights.

Saving Models with PyTorch

PyTorch offers flexibility in saving models by allowing developers to save the entire model or just the state dictionary (parameters). Here's how:

```python
import torch
import torch.nn as nn

# Define a simple model
class SimpleModel(nn.Module):
    def __init__(self):
        super(SimpleModel, self).__init__()
        self.fc = nn.Linear(1, 1)

    def forward(self, x):
        return self.fc(x)

# Initialize and train the model
model = SimpleModel()
optimizer = torch.optim.SGD(model.parameters(), lr=0.01)
criterion = nn.MSELoss()
x = torch.tensor([[1.0], [2.0], [3.0]])
y = torch.tensor([[2.0], [4.0], [6.0]])
for epoch in range(100):
    optimizer.zero_grad()
    output = model(x)
    loss = criterion(output, y)
    loss.backward()
    optimizer.step()

# Save the model
torch.save(model.state_dict(), 'simple_model.pth')

# Load the model
loaded_model = SimpleModel()
loaded_model.load_state_dict(torch.load('simple_model.pth'))
loaded_model.eval()
print("Loaded model prediction:", loaded_model(torch.tensor([[4.0]])))
```

PyTorch's state_dict provides a compact and efficient way to save only the essential parameters of the model.

Best Practices for Exporting Models

1. **Choose the Right Format**: Select a format based on compatibility and future use cases.
2. **Document the Model**: Include metadata such as model version, training data, and parameters.
3. **Test After Loading**: Always test the loaded model to ensure its integrity.
4. **Compress Large Models**: Use compression techniques to save storage and enhance portability.

Exporting and saving models is a fundamental practice in machine learning and AI workflows. By leveraging the capabilities of scikit-learn, TensorFlow, and PyTorch, developers can ensure their models are ready for deployment, collaboration, and further analysis. Embracing best practices in this area enhances the reproducibility, efficiency, and robustness of AI systems.

Building Flask APIs for AI Predictions

Flask is a lightweight and versatile Python web framework that makes it simple to create RESTful APIs. By integrating AI models with Flask, developers can efficiently serve predictions through HTTP endpoints. This capability is essential for building scalable, real-time prediction systems that can be accessed by various clients, such as web applications, mobile apps, or IoT devices.

Integrating AI Models with Flask

| Create Flask API | Integrate AI Model | Serve Predictions | Access by Clients |

Why Use Flask for AI Predictions?

- **Lightweight Framework**: Flask's minimalistic nature allows for rapid development and deployment.
- **Flexibility**: Its modular design supports adding features as needed.
- **Integration-Friendly**: Easily integrates with machine learning models and tools like joblib, TensorFlow, and PyTorch.
- **Wide Adoption**: Supported by a large community and extensive documentation.

Setting Up a Flask API for AI Predictions

Below is an example of building a Flask API that serves predictions using a pre-trained model.

Example: Flask API for Model Deployment

```
from flask import Flask, request, jsonify
import joblib

# Load the pre-trained model
```

```python
model = joblib.load('linear_regression_model.pkl')

# Create Flask app
app = Flask(__name__)

@app.route('/predict', methods=['POST'])
def predict():
    try:
        # Parse incoming JSON data
        data = request.get_json()
        features = data['features']

        # Make prediction
        prediction = model.predict([features]).tolist()

        # Return prediction as JSON
        return jsonify({'prediction': prediction})
    except Exception as e:
        return jsonify({'error': str(e)}), 400

if __name__ == '__main__':
    app.run(debug=True)
```

Key Features of the Code:

1. **Model Loading**: The pre-trained model is loaded using joblib.load, ensuring consistency with the training pipeline.
2. **API Route**: A POST endpoint (/predict) is defined to handle prediction requests.
3. **Input Handling**: The API parses input features from JSON data sent in the request body.
4. **Error Handling**: Basic error handling is implemented to return meaningful messages for invalid inputs or issues.

5. **Flask Development Server**: The app runs on a local development server with debugging enabled.

Steps to Deploy the Flask API

1. **Prepare the Model**:
    - Train your machine learning model using libraries like scikit-learn, TensorFlow, or PyTorch.
    - Save the trained model using joblib or pickle to ensure compatibility during deployment.
2. **Set Up Flask**:
    - Install Flask using pip:
    - pip install flask
    - Create a Python script with defined API routes and endpoints.
3. **Test Locally**:
    - Run the Flask app locally to test API functionality:
    - python app.py
    - Use tools like Postman or cURL to send POST requests with JSON payloads.
4. **Deploy to Production**:
    - **Local Deployment**: Use a production-ready WSGI server like Gunicorn or uWSGI for serving the app.
    - **Cloud Deployment**:
        - Deploy on platforms like Heroku, AWS Elastic Beanstalk, Google Cloud Run, or Microsoft Azure.
        - Dockerize the application for container-based deployment.

5. **Secure the API**:
    - Implement authentication mechanisms (e.g., API keys, OAuth).
    - Use HTTPS to encrypt data in transit.
    - Apply rate limiting to prevent abuse.
6. **Monitor and Maintain**:
    - Use monitoring tools like Prometheus or New Relic to track API performance.
    - Log requests and errors for troubleshooting and analytics.

Enhancements and Best Practices

- **Scalability**:
    - Use a load balancer to handle high traffic.
    - Deploy the API on scalable platforms like AWS Lambda for serverless execution.
- **Input Validation**:
    - Validate incoming data to ensure compatibility with the model.
    - Use libraries like Marshmallow or Pydantic for schema validation.
- **Batch Predictions**:
    - Extend the API to handle batch predictions for improved efficiency in bulk processing scenarios.
- **Comprehensive Testing**:
    - Write unit tests and integration tests to validate API functionality and ensure robustness.
- **API Documentation**:
    - Document API endpoints using tools like Swagger or Postman.

- Include examples of input payloads and expected responses.

Building Flask APIs for AI predictions bridges the gap between trained models and real-world applications. By following the steps outlined above, you can create a robust and scalable API that serves predictions to clients efficiently. Leveraging Flask's simplicity and Python's extensive machine learning ecosystem ensures a smooth development experience, enabling you to focus on delivering actionable insights through AI.

Deploying AI Models Using Streamlit

Streamlit is an open-source Python library specifically designed to create interactive and visually appealing web applications with minimal effort. It is a perfect choice for deploying AI models because it enables developers to quickly build user interfaces without requiring extensive web development experience. By combining Streamlit's intuitive design with Python's robust machine learning libraries, you can deliver dynamic and interactive AI-powered web applications.

Why Choose Streamlit for AI Model Deployment?

1. **Ease of Use**: Streamlit simplifies the process of creating web interfaces by eliminating the need for front-end frameworks like HTML, CSS, or JavaScript.
2. **Rapid Prototyping**: Developers can iterate quickly and view updates in real time, enabling faster deployment cycles.

3. **Interactivity**: Provides a range of widgets such as sliders, text inputs, and buttons to make applications interactive.
4. **Visualization**: Easily integrates with popular Python visualization libraries like Matplotlib, Plotly, and Seaborn to display data and model predictions.
5. **Open Source and Free**: No licensing costs, making it an ideal choice for hobbyists, researchers, and professionals.

Setting Up a Streamlit Application

Below is an example of deploying a machine learning model using Streamlit.

Example: Deploying a Model with Streamlit

```
import streamlit as st
import joblib

# Load the model
model = joblib.load('linear_regression_model.pkl')

# Create a Streamlit app
st.title("AI Model Deployment with Streamlit")

# Input features
feature = st.number_input("Enter a feature value:")

# Predict button
if st.button("Predict"):
    prediction = model.predict([[feature]])[0]
    st.write(f"Prediction: {prediction}")
```

Step-by-Step Guide to Deploy with Streamlit

1. **Install Streamlit**: Install Streamlit using pip:

   pip install streamlit

2. **Write the Application Script**: Create a Python script (e.g., app.py) that includes Streamlit components such as:
   - **st.title**: For adding a title to your application.
   - **st.input** and **st.number_input**: For capturing user input.
   - **st.write**: For displaying output and results.
3. **Run the Application**: Launch the Streamlit app using the following command:

   streamlit run app.py

   This will start a local web server and open the application in your default browser.

4. **Test the Application**: Ensure the app behaves as expected by entering various inputs and verifying the predictions.
5. **Deploy the Application**:
   - **Streamlit Cloud**: Use Streamlit's free hosting platform for easy sharing.
   - **Cloud Platforms**: Deploy on platforms like AWS, Google Cloud, or Azure using Docker containers.
   - **Self-Hosting**: Deploy the app on your own server using tools like Nginx or Gunicorn.

Enhancing Your Streamlit Application

Add More Widgets

Streamlit supports various interactive widgets to enhance user experience:

- **Sliders**:

    ```
    feature = st.slider("Select a feature value:", min_value=0.0, max_value=100.0, step=0.1)
    ```

- **File Uploads**: Allow users to upload datasets for batch predictions:

    ```
    uploaded_file = st.file_uploader("Upload a CSV file")
    ```

- **Dropdowns**: Enable users to choose options:

    ```
    option = st.selectbox("Select an option:", ["Option 1", "Option 2", "Option 3"])
    ```

Add Visualizations

Visualize data and predictions with libraries like Matplotlib and Plotly:

- **Matplotlib Example**:

    ```
    import matplotlib.pyplot as plt
    fig, ax = plt.subplots()
    ax.plot([1, 2, 3], [1, 4, 9])
    st.pyplot(fig)
    ```

- **Plotly Example**:

```python
import plotly.express as px
fig = px.scatter(x=[1, 2, 3], y=[1, 4, 9])
st.plotly_chart(fig)
```

Improve Model Outputs

Provide confidence intervals or additional metrics:

- Show probabilities for classification models.
- Display feature importance for interpretability.

Best Practices for Streamlit Deployment

1. **Optimize Model Size**: Compress large models or use quantized versions for faster loading.
2. **Secure the Application**:
   - Add authentication mechanisms to restrict access.
   - Use HTTPS to secure data in transit.
3. **Scalability**:
   - Containerize the app using Docker for consistent deployment.
   - Use load balancers to handle increased traffic.
4. **Documentation**:
   - Provide clear instructions for users on how to interact with the app.
   - Include examples of input data and expected results.

Streamlit is an excellent tool for deploying AI models with interactive and user-friendly interfaces. Its simplicity, combined with Python's machine learning capabilities, makes it a go-to choice for developers and data scientists.

By following the outlined steps and best practices, you can create powerful applications that bring your AI models to life, enabling real-time predictions and impactful user experiences.

10. Ethics and Challenges in AI Development

As artificial intelligence (AI) continues to evolve and deeply integrate into various industries, its transformative potential is accompanied by complex ethical implications and challenges. The growing reliance on AI for decision-making, automation, and personalized experiences has magnified the importance of addressing these concerns holistically. Mitigating biases, ensuring robust data privacy mechanisms, and adhering to ethical principles are not just technical challenges but societal imperatives. Developing responsible AI systems requires an approach that combines technical innovation with an unwavering commitment to fairness, transparency, and accountability. This chapter explores these multifaceted dimensions in depth, providing actionable strategies, real-world examples, and practical insights to help developers and organizations design AI systems that align with ethical standards and serve humanity equitably.

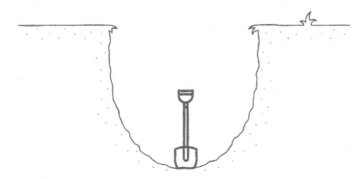

Ethical AI issues lead to biases and privacy risks.

Mitigating Bias in AI Models

Bias in AI models occurs when the outcomes disproportionately favor or disadvantage certain groups due to imbalances in the training data, flawed algorithms, or unintentional developer assumptions. This issue can lead to unfair decisions, perpetuate stereotypes, and undermine the credibility of AI systems.

Types of Bias in AI

1. **Data Bias**:
   - **Definition**: Arises from imbalanced or non-representative training datasets.
   - **Example**: A facial recognition system trained predominantly on light-skinned individuals may fail to recognize darker-skinned faces accurately.
2. **Algorithmic Bias**:
   - **Definition**: Occurs when algorithms amplify or create disparities based on their design.
   - **Example**: Recommendation engines that reinforce echo chambers by suggesting content similar to users' previous interactions.
3. **Human Bias**:
   - **Definition**: Results from developers' unconscious biases during dataset selection or algorithm design.

Strategies to Mitigate Bias

1. **Diversify Training Data:**

- **Approach**: Use datasets that reflect the diversity of the target population.
- **Enhancement**: Incorporate synthetic data to address underrepresented groups.

2. **Bias Audits**:
   - **Objective**: Perform regular audits using fairness metrics such as demographic parity, equalized odds, or disparate impact.
   - **Example Code for Bias Detection in Python**:

   ```python
   from sklearn.metrics import confusion_matrix

   def evaluate_fairness(predictions, labels, group_attribute):
       cm = confusion_matrix(labels, predictions)
       fairness_score = cm[1][1] / sum(cm[:, 1])  # Positive predictive value for a specific group
       return fairness_score
   ```

3. **Algorithmic Fairness Techniques**:
   - **Implementation**: Use fairness-aware algorithms such as reweighting techniques or adversarial debiasing.
   - **Toolkits**: Libraries like AIF360 provide tools for mitigating bias in machine learning pipelines.

4. **Stakeholder Collaboration**:
   - **Engagement**: Involve diverse stakeholders to identify and address potential biases during development.

5. **Transparency and Explainability**:
   - **Purpose**: Employ interpretable models and provide explanations for decisions to ensure accountability.

Why Addressing Bias is Crucial

Mitigating bias in AI systems is not merely a technical necessity but also a moral and societal imperative. Unbiased AI systems foster trust among users, promote equitable treatment, and ensure compliance with ethical and legal standards. Addressing bias ensures AI systems can be reliably deployed across sensitive domains such as healthcare, hiring, and law enforcement.

Challenges in Mitigating Bias

1. **Dataset Limitations**:
    - Even with diverse datasets, achieving true representation can be difficult due to historical data imbalances.
2. **Complexity of Fairness Metrics**:
    - Balancing multiple fairness metrics may lead to trade-offs, complicating model evaluation.
3. **Continuous Monitoring**:
    - Models deployed in dynamic environments require ongoing audits to adapt to evolving societal norms.

Future Directions

1. **Advanced Synthetic Data Generation**:
    - Leveraging generative AI to create high-quality, diverse datasets.
2. **Legislation and Standards**:
    - Development of industry-wide standards and regulations for fairness in AI.

3. **Education and Awareness**:
    - Equipping AI developers with the knowledge to recognize and mitigate bias effectively.

By adopting a holistic approach to identifying and addressing bias, AI practitioners can build systems that are not only technologically robust but also ethically sound, fostering greater societal acceptance and trust.

Ensuring Data Privacy in Python Applications

Data privacy is a cornerstone of ethical AI development. As AI systems rely heavily on vast amounts of data, safeguarding this information is paramount to building trust and complying with legal regulations like GDPR (General Data Protection Regulation) and CCPA (California Consumer Privacy Act).

Ensuring Data Privacy in AI

Principles of Data Privacy

1. **Minimization**:

- **Definition**: Collect only the data necessary for the task at hand.
- **Example**: If an application requires a user's email address for communication, avoid collecting additional data like their physical address unless essential.

2. **Anonymization**:
   - **Definition**: Remove identifiable information to protect user identities.
   - **Techniques**: Utilize pseudonymization or randomization methods to ensure that individual data cannot be traced back to specific users.
3. **Transparency**:
   - **Definition**: Clearly communicate how data is collected, stored, processed, and used.
   - **Best Practices**: Provide users with an easy-to-understand privacy policy and update them about changes proactively.
4. **Consent**:
   - **Definition**: Obtain explicit consent before collecting sensitive information.
   - **Implementation**: Use clear, opt-in mechanisms for users to agree to data collection, ensuring compliance with privacy laws.

Implementing Privacy Measures in Python

1. **Data Encryption**:
   - **Purpose**: Protect sensitive data from unauthorized access.

- **Implementation**: Use libraries like PyCryptodome for encryption and decryption of sensitive data.

    ```
    from Crypto.Cipher import AES

    key = b'mysecretencryptionkey'
    cipher = AES.new(key, AES.MODE_EAX)
    ciphertext, tag = cipher.encrypt_and_digest(b'Sensitive Data')
    print(f"Encrypted Data: {ciphertext}")
    ```

2. **Data Masking**:
    - **Purpose**: Replace sensitive data with placeholders during processing.
    - **Example Code**:

        ```
        def mask_data(data, mask_char="*"):
            return mask_char * len(data)

        print(mask_data("123-45-6789"))  # Output: *********
        ```

3. **Secure APIs**:
    - **Techniques**: Implement HTTPS for secure communication and use authentication mechanisms like OAuth to validate API requests.
    - **Frameworks**: Use Python frameworks like Flask or FastAPI with security plugins to ensure API robustness.
4. **Federated Learning**:
    - **Definition**: Train models locally on user devices to avoid transmitting raw data to centralized servers.

- **Advantages**: Reduces the risk of data breaches and ensures compliance with data localization laws.
5. **Privacy-Preserving Techniques**:
    - **Differential Privacy**:
        - Adds noise to datasets to prevent identification of individual records.
        - **Example Code**:

        ```
        import numpy as np

        def add_differential_noise(data, epsilon=1.0):
            noise = np.random.laplace(0, 1/epsilon, size=len(data))
            return data + noise
        ```

    - **Homomorphic Encryption**:
        - Allows computations on encrypted data without needing to decrypt it first, maintaining privacy throughout the process.
6. **Access Controls**:
    - **Implementation**: Use role-based access controls (RBAC) to ensure that only authorized users can access specific datasets.

Best Practices for Privacy Compliance

1. **Conduct Regular Audits**:
    - Regularly review your application's data handling practices and ensure compliance with evolving regulations.
2. **User Education**:

- Inform users about their data rights, such as the right to access, delete, or correct their data.
3. **Data Retention Policies**:
    - Define clear policies on how long data will be retained and ensure secure deletion of data no longer needed.
4. **Incident Response Plan**:
    - Develop a robust plan to respond to data breaches, including notification protocols and mitigation strategies.

Challenges in Ensuring Data Privacy

1. **Evolving Regulations**:
    - Privacy laws like GDPR and CCPA are updated frequently, requiring continuous monitoring and adaptation.
2. **Balancing Utility and Privacy**:
    - Adding noise or anonymizing data can reduce its utility for AI models, creating trade-offs between accuracy and privacy.
3. **Third-Party Integrations**:
    - Ensuring privacy compliance when using external services or APIs can be challenging and requires additional diligence.

Future Directions in Data Privacy

1. **Zero-Knowledge Proofs**:
    - A cryptographic method that enables proving information without revealing the information itself.

2. **Privacy-First Development**:
   o Incorporating privacy as a design principle from the earliest stages of software development.
3. **AI-Driven Privacy Solutions**:
   o Leveraging AI to monitor and manage privacy risks dynamically.

By adopting robust privacy measures and adhering to ethical guidelines, Python developers can build applications that not only comply with legal standards but also foster user trust and confidence in AI systems.

Real-World Considerations for Ethical AI

Developing ethical AI extends beyond mitigating bias and ensuring privacy; it requires addressing broader societal implications and real-world challenges. To create systems that are responsible, equitable, and trusted, developers must integrate ethical considerations into every stage of AI development and deployment.

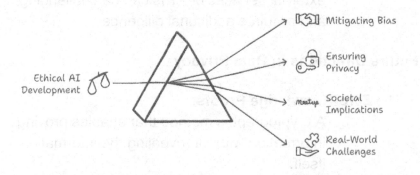

Unpacking Ethical AI: A Multifaceted Approach

Key Considerations for Ethical AI

1. **Accountability**:
   - **Definition**: Define clear accountability frameworks for AI decisions and outcomes.
   - **Implementation**: Assign responsibilities for errors or unintended consequences, whether they arise from model behavior, data biases, or deployment settings.
   - **Example**: Establishing a team responsible for investigating AI system errors and communicating findings transparently.
2. **Accessibility**:
   - **Goal**: Ensure AI technologies are inclusive and accessible to all users, regardless of socioeconomic status, geographic location, or abilities.
   - **Approach**: Design interfaces that accommodate users with disabilities, such as voice recognition for visually impaired users or multilingual support.
   - **Example**: Deploying AI-powered educational tools in underserved communities to bridge the digital divide.
3. **Environmental Impact**:
   - **Challenge**: AI systems, particularly large language models, consume significant computational resources and energy.
   - **Solutions**:
     - Optimize algorithms to reduce energy consumption.

- Explore green AI initiatives that prioritize sustainability, such as using renewable energy for data centers.
  - **Example**: Implementing pruning and quantization techniques to reduce the size of neural networks without sacrificing performance.
4. **Legal and Regulatory Compliance**:
   - **Necessity**: Stay updated on regional and international AI regulations, including GDPR, CCPA, and emerging frameworks like the EU's AI Act.
   - **Action Steps**:
     - Document compliance efforts and maintain audit trails.
     - Conduct regular reviews to ensure adherence to legal standards.
   - **Example**: Ensuring transparency by providing users with detailed documentation on how their data is used and processed.
5. **Continuous Monitoring**:
   - **Rationale**: AI systems operate in dynamic environments and can be influenced by changing societal norms, values, or external threats.
   - **Approach**:
     - Regularly update models to address new ethical concerns and technological developments.
     - Monitor systems post-deployment to identify and address unforeseen issues.

- Example: Conducting bias audits periodically and retraining models to reflect evolving societal perspectives.

6. **Public Awareness**:
   - **Objective**: Educate users about AI capabilities, limitations, and ethical considerations.
   - **Methods**:
     - Use clear, jargon-free communication to foster trust.
     - Provide interactive tools that allow users to understand AI decision-making processes.
   - **Example**: Hosting workshops or creating explainer videos that demystify AI technologies for the general public.

Ethical AI in Action: A Case Study

An AI-powered hiring platform was designed to screen job applications and identify the most suitable candidates. While efficient, the system inadvertently favored male applicants due to historical biases in training data. To address this:

1. **Bias Mitigation**:
   - Implemented fairness-aware algorithms to reduce gender bias.
   - Conducted regular audits to evaluate hiring patterns.
2. **Transparency**:
   - Provided applicants with insights into how their profiles were evaluated.
3. **Accountability**:

- Assigned a dedicated team to address complaints and continuously refine the system.

By taking these steps, the company ensured a fairer and more ethical recruitment process.

Challenges in Ethical AI Development

1. **Balancing Competing Priorities**:
   - Ethical considerations often compete with business goals like profitability or speed-to-market.
2. **Global Variations in Ethical Standards**:
   - Ethical norms and regulations differ across regions, complicating AI deployment in global markets.
3. **Complexity of Ethical Metrics**:
   - Measuring fairness, accountability, or accessibility can be subjective and context-dependent.

Future Directions for Ethical AI

1. **Collaborative Governance**:
   - Foster collaboration between governments, private sectors, and academia to create unified ethical standards.
2. **AI Explainability**:
   - Invest in research to develop interpretable models that allow stakeholders to understand AI decision-making.
3. **Decentralized AI Development**:

- Explore federated learning and other decentralized approaches to minimize data centralization and enhance privacy.

The Role of Developers in Ethical AI

Developers are at the forefront of ethical AI. By integrating ethical principles into the design, training, and deployment of AI systems, they can:

- Promote fairness and inclusivity.
- Build trust and credibility with users.
- Ensure compliance with evolving legal and societal expectations.

Ethical AI development is not a one-time effort but an ongoing commitment to fairness, privacy, and societal well-being. By addressing these considerations, developers can create AI systems that serve humanity responsibly and equitably.

11. End-to-End AI Projects in Python

AI is rapidly transforming industries by introducing innovative solutions that revolutionize how tasks are performed and decisions are made. The practical application of AI through real-world projects is essential for gaining hands-on experience and understanding the nuances of development and deployment. This section delves into a diverse array of end-to-end AI projects, each meticulously designed to address specific challenges across various domains. Each project illustrates advanced techniques, cutting-edge libraries, and modern approaches widely recognized in AI development, ensuring a comprehensive learning experience for developers and enthusiasts alike.

Project 1: Predicting Stock Market Trends

Objective:

To develop a machine learning model capable of predicting stock prices based on historical data. The primary goal is to provide users with actionable insights to inform investment decisions by leveraging data-driven techniques.

Detailed Plan:
1. Data Collection:

- Utilize APIs such as Alpha Vantage, Yahoo Finance, or Quandl to gather historical stock market data.
- Ensure data includes relevant features such as opening price, closing price, high, low, trading

volume, and other market indicators (e.g., moving averages or sentiment scores).
- Store the data in a structured format, such as CSV or directly into a database for ease of processing.

2. Data Preprocessing:

- Handle missing values using interpolation or other statistical techniques.
- Normalize or scale features to ensure consistency, especially for machine learning models that are sensitive to input ranges.
- Engineer new features, such as daily returns, volatility indices, and technical indicators like RSI (Relative Strength Index) or MACD (Moving Average Convergence Divergence).

3. Exploratory Data Analysis (EDA):

- Visualize trends and patterns over time using libraries such as Matplotlib and Seaborn.
- Identify correlations between various indicators and stock price movements.
- Use time-series decomposition to separate data into trend, seasonal, and residual components.
- Detect outliers or anomalies that could impact model performance.

4. Model Selection and Training:

- For time-series forecasting, consider models such as:

- **LSTMs (Long Short-Term Memory networks):** Ideal for capturing sequential dependencies and long-term trends in stock prices.
- **ARIMA (AutoRegressive Integrated Moving Average):** Effective for linear time-series data with trend and seasonality.
  - Experiment with hybrid models combining traditional statistical techniques with deep learning for improved accuracy.
  - Split data into training, validation, and test sets to evaluate performance.

5. Model Evaluation:

- Use metrics such as Mean Absolute Error (MAE), Root Mean Squared Error (RMSE), and Mean Absolute Percentage Error (MAPE) to gauge model accuracy.
- Perform backtesting by simulating predictions on historical data and comparing them to actual outcomes.
- Incorporate cross-validation techniques to ensure robustness across different market conditions.

6. Deployment:

- Create a user-friendly dashboard or application where users can input parameters (e.g., stock ticker, date range) and receive predictions.

- Use frameworks like Flask or Django for backend development and integrate with APIs for real-time data retrieval.
- Ensure scalability and reliability of the application for handling multiple users and large datasets.

7. Post-Deployment Monitoring:

- Continuously monitor model performance and retrain periodically with new data.
- Incorporate user feedback to enhance prediction accuracy and usability.
- Add additional features like sentiment analysis from news or social media to refine predictions.

Outcome:

By following this systematic approach, the project aims to provide users with reliable stock price predictions. These insights can help investors make informed decisions, manage risk, and optimize portfolio performance. Additionally, the project demonstrates the practical application of machine learning and time-series analysis in financial markets, paving the way for advanced analytical tools in the investment domain.

Example Code:

```
import pandas as pd
import numpy as np
import matplotlib.pyplot as plt
import seaborn as sns
from sklearn.preprocessing import MinMaxScaler
from keras.models import Sequential
```

```python
from keras.layers import LSTM, Dense
from sklearn.metrics import mean_squared_error
from math import sqrt

# Step 1: Data Collection
# Assuming data is downloaded as a CSV file
data = pd.read_csv('historical_stock_data.csv')
data['Date'] = pd.to_datetime(data['Date'])
data.set_index('Date', inplace=True)

# Step 2: Data Preprocessing
scaler = MinMaxScaler(feature_range=(0, 1))
data_scaled = scaler.fit_transform(data[['Close']])

# Create sequences for LSTM
def create_sequences(data, seq_length):
    sequences, targets = [], []
    for i in range(len(data) - seq_length):
        sequences.append(data[i:i+seq_length])
        targets.append(data[i+seq_length])
    return np.array(sequences), np.array(targets)

seq_length = 60
X, y = create_sequences(data_scaled, seq_length)

# Split into train and test
split = int(0.8 * len(X))
X_train, X_test = X[:split], X[split:]
y_train, y_test = y[:split], y[split:]

# Step 3: Model Training
model = Sequential([
    LSTM(50, return_sequences=True, input_shape=(seq_length, 1)),
    LSTM(50, return_sequences=False),
    Dense(25),
    Dense(1)
])
```

```
model.compile(optimizer='adam', loss='mean_squared_error')
model.fit(X_train, y_train, batch_size=32, epochs=10)

# Step 4: Model Evaluation
predictions = model.predict(X_test)
rmse = sqrt(mean_squared_error(y_test, predictions))
print(f'RMSE: {rmse}')

# Step 5: Visualization
plt.figure(figsize=(10, 6))
plt.plot(data.index[-len(y_test):], scaler.inverse_transform(y_test), label='True Prices')
plt.plot(data.index[-len(predictions):], scaler.inverse_transform(predictions), label='Predicted Prices')
plt.legend()
plt.show()
```

Project 2: Real-Time Face Recognition with OpenCV

Objective:

To develop a system that can identify and recognize faces in real-time using a webcam or video feed. This system can serve various purposes, including security, attendance management, or personal use, by leveraging state-of-the-art face recognition technologies.

Detailed Plan:
1. Face Detection:

- Use OpenCV's cv2.CascadeClassifier to detect faces in real-time video frames.

- Employ pre-trained Haar cascades or DNN-based detectors for enhanced accuracy and performance.
- Ensure the system is optimized for different lighting conditions and camera angles.

2. Feature Extraction:

- Integrate deep learning models like FaceNet or dlib's ResNet-based face recognition module for feature extraction.
- Generate 128-dimensional face embeddings to uniquely identify individuals.
- Store these embeddings in a database or file system for comparison.

3. Face Recognition:

- Use a similarity metric (e.g., cosine similarity or Euclidean distance) to match real-time face embeddings with stored embeddings.
- Implement multi-threading or asynchronous processing to enhance real-time performance.

4. Performance Optimization:

- Leverage GPU acceleration using libraries like CUDA for faster frame processing.
- Optimize frame rates to ensure smooth operation without sacrificing accuracy.
- Implement techniques like face alignment to improve recognition reliability.

5. User-Friendly Features:

- Add face labeling to display the names of recognized individuals on the video feed.
- Include an attendance tracking module that logs the entry and exit times of individuals.
- Provide a GUI or web interface for ease of use and interaction.

6. Testing and Deployment:

- Test the system under various real-world conditions, including crowded environments and diverse lighting scenarios.
- Deploy the application on different platforms, such as PCs, Raspberry Pi, or cloud-based servers, depending on use cases.

Outcome:

A robust real-time face recognition system that can be used for applications in security, attendance tracking, and more. This project demonstrates the practical use of computer vision and deep learning in creating intelligent, real-time systems.

Example Code:

```
import cv2
import numpy as np
import face_recognition
from datetime import datetime

# Step 1: Load Known Faces and Encodings
```

```python
known_face_encodings = []
known_face_names = []

# Load sample images and encode faces
known_image = face_recognition.load_image_file('person1.jpg')
known_encoding = face_recognition.face_encodings(known_image)[0]
known_face_encodings.append(known_encoding)
known_face_names.append('Person 1')

# Step 2: Initialize Webcam
video_capture = cv2.VideoCapture(0)

# Step 3: Process Each Frame
while True:
    ret, frame = video_capture.read()
    rgb_frame = frame[:, :, ::-1]

    # Detect Faces
    face_locations = face_recognition.face_locations(rgb_frame)
    face_encodings = face_recognition.face_encodings(rgb_frame, face_locations)

    # Match Faces
    for (top, right, bottom, left), face_encoding in zip(face_locations, face_encodings):
        matches = face_recognition.compare_faces(known_face_encodings, face_encoding)
        name = "Unknown"

        # Use the first match
        if True in matches:
            match_index = matches.index(True)
            name = known_face_names[match_index]

        # Display Label
        cv2.rectangle(frame, (left, top), (right, bottom), (0, 255, 0), 2)
```

```
        cv2.putText(frame, name, (left, top - 10),
cv2.FONT_HERSHEY_SIMPLEX, 0.9, (0, 255, 0), 2)

    # Show Frame
    cv2.imshow('Video', frame)

    # Exit on 'q'
    if cv2.waitKey(1) & 0xFF == ord('q'):
        break

# Release Resources
video_capture.release()
cv2.destroyAllWindows()
```

Project 3: Sentiment Analysis for Customer Feedback

Objective:

To analyze customer reviews and feedback to identify sentiments as positive, neutral, or negative. The project aims to empower businesses to understand customer opinions at scale and prioritize improvements effectively.

Detailed Plan:

1. Data Collection:

- Gather customer reviews from platforms such as Amazon, Twitter, or company websites.
- Use web scraping tools like BeautifulSoup or Scrapy to extract review data if APIs are unavailable.
- Include fields like review text, rating, timestamp, and user details for comprehensive analysis.

2. Data Preprocessing:

   - Remove noise such as HTML tags, special characters, and URLs from the text.
   - Convert all text to lowercase for uniformity.
   - Tokenize the text and remove stopwords using libraries like NLTK or spaCy.
   - Perform stemming or lemmatization to standardize words.
   - Create a labeled dataset if necessary by tagging reviews manually or using pre-labeled datasets.

3. Model Training:

   - Explore machine learning models such as Logistic Regression, Naïve Bayes, and Support Vector Machines for basic sentiment classification.
   - Utilize pre-trained models from Hugging Face's Transformers library (e.g., BERT, DistilBERT) for advanced natural language processing.
   - Fine-tune models on the collected dataset to improve accuracy and relevance.

4. Evaluation Metrics:

   - Use accuracy, precision, recall, and F1-score to measure model performance.
   - Perform cross-validation to ensure the robustness of results.

5. Visualization and Insights:

   - Create dashboards using tools like Plotly, Tableau, or Power BI to display sentiment trends over time.
   - Visualize key insights such as the percentage of positive, neutral, and negative reviews.
   - Highlight frequently mentioned keywords and topics associated with specific sentiments.

6. Deployment:

   - Develop a web-based or desktop application for sentiment analysis.
   - Allow users to input customer feedback or upload files for batch analysis.
   - Integrate APIs for real-time sentiment prediction.

7. Scalability and Optimization:

   - Use cloud services like AWS or Google Cloud for scalable data storage and model deployment.
   - Implement parallel processing or GPU acceleration for faster analysis of large datasets.

Outcome:

By implementing this project, businesses can gain actionable insights into customer sentiments, enabling them to improve products, services, and customer experiences. Sentiment analysis provides a scalable way to monitor brand reputation and address concerns proactively.

Example Code:

```python
import pandas as pd
import numpy as np
import re
from sklearn.model_selection import train_test_split
from sklearn.feature_extraction.text import CountVectorizer
from sklearn.naive_bayes import MultinomialNB
from sklearn.metrics import classification_report, accuracy_score

# Step 1: Load Data
data = pd.read_csv('customer_reviews.csv')
data['cleaned_reviews'] = data['review'].apply(lambda x: re.sub(r'[^a-zA-Z\s]', '', x).lower())

# Step 2: Split Data
X_train, X_test, y_train, y_test = train_test_split(
    data['cleaned_reviews'], data['sentiment'], test_size=0.2, random_state=42
)

# Step 3: Vectorize Text
vectorizer = CountVectorizer(stop_words='english')
X_train_vectorized = vectorizer.fit_transform(X_train)
X_test_vectorized = vectorizer.transform(X_test)

# Step 4: Train Model
model = MultinomialNB()
model.fit(X_train_vectorized, y_train)

# Step 5: Evaluate Model
predictions = model.predict(X_test_vectorized)
print(classification_report(y_test, predictions))
print(f'Accuracy: {accuracy_score(y_test, predictions)}')

# Step 6: Real-Time Prediction
new_review = ["The product was excellent and exceeded expectations."]
new_review_vectorized = vectorizer.transform(new_review)
print(f"Predicted Sentiment: {model.predict(new_review_vectorized)[0]}")
```

Project 4: Image Classification with CNNs

Objective:

To classify images into predefined categories using Convolutional Neural Networks (CNNs). This project demonstrates the power of deep learning in various domains, including quality control, healthcare, and retail.

Detailed Plan:

1. Dataset Selection:

- Use publicly available datasets like CIFAR-10 (for small object categories) or ImageNet (for large-scale image classification).
- Split the dataset into training, validation, and test sets to ensure robust evaluation.
- Optionally, collect domain-specific data and annotate it using tools like LabelImg for custom applications.

2. Data Preprocessing:

- Resize images to a consistent input size (e.g., 32x32 for CIFAR-10 or 224x224 for ImageNet).
- Normalize pixel values to a range of [0, 1] or [-1, 1].
- Apply data augmentation techniques such as flipping, rotation, scaling, and cropping to enhance generalization.

3. Model Building:

- Design a CNN architecture using frameworks like TensorFlow or PyTorch. For instance:
    - Input Layer: Accepts image data.
    - Convolutional Layers: Extract spatial features using filters.
    - Pooling Layers: Reduce spatial dimensions and computation.
    - Fully Connected Layers: Map extracted features to output categories.
- Use transfer learning with pre-trained models like ResNet, VGG, or EfficientNet for faster training and improved performance.

4. Model Training:

- Define a loss function, such as categorical cross-entropy, and an optimizer like Adam or SGD.
- Train the model on the training set while validating on the validation set to prevent overfitting.
- Use callbacks like early stopping and learning rate scheduling to optimize the training process.

5. Performance Evaluation:

- Evaluate the model using metrics like accuracy, precision, recall, and F1-score on the test set.
- Generate a confusion matrix to analyze classification errors.
- Perform error analysis to identify and address misclassifications.

6. Deployment:

- Deploy the model using frameworks like Flask or FastAPI to create a REST API.
- Integrate the model into a web or mobile application for real-world usage.
- Use platforms like TensorFlow Serving or TorchServe for efficient model serving.

7. Scalability and Optimization:

- Optimize the model for inference using TensorRT or ONNX.
- Use cloud platforms like AWS, GCP, or Azure for scalable deployment.
- Enable batch processing for handling multiple requests simultaneously.

Outcome:

By implementing this project, you will build a powerful image classification system that can be applied to various industries, including manufacturing (quality control), healthcare (disease detection), and retail (product categorization). The project demonstrates the capabilities of CNNs and transfer learning in solving real-world problems.

Example Code:

```
import tensorflow as tf
from tensorflow.keras.models import Sequential
from tensorflow.keras.layers import Conv2D, MaxPooling2D, Flatten, Dense, Dropout
from tensorflow.keras.preprocessing.image import ImageDataGenerator
```

```python
# Step 1: Load and Preprocess Data
(train_images, train_labels), (test_images, test_labels) = tf.keras.datasets.cifar10.load_data()
train_images, test_images = train_images / 255.0, test_images / 255.0

# Step 2: Data Augmentation
datagen = ImageDataGenerator(
    rotation_range=15,
    width_shift_range=0.1,
    height_shift_range=0.1,
    horizontal_flip=True
)
datagen.fit(train_images)

# Step 3: Build CNN Model
model = Sequential([
    Conv2D(32, (3, 3), activation='relu', input_shape=(32, 32, 3)),
    MaxPooling2D((2, 2)),
    Conv2D(64, (3, 3), activation='relu'),
    MaxPooling2D((2, 2)),
    Flatten(),
    Dense(128, activation='relu'),
    Dropout(0.5),
    Dense(10, activation='softmax')
])

# Step 4: Compile Model
model.compile(optimizer='adam',
              loss='sparse_categorical_crossentropy',
              metrics=['accuracy'])

# Step 5: Train Model
model.fit(datagen.flow(train_images, train_labels, batch_size=64),
          epochs=10, validation_data=(test_images, test_labels))

# Step 6: Evaluate Model
test_loss, test_accuracy = model.evaluate(test_images, test_labels)
```

```
print(f"Test Accuracy: {test_accuracy * 100:.2f}%")

# Step 7: Save and Deploy Model
model.save('image_classification_model.h5')
```

Project 5: Text Summarization with NLP

Objective:

To create a tool that generates concise and coherent summaries from lengthy documents, articles, or other textual content. The project aims to save users time by distilling key information and presenting it in a clear and understandable format. Additionally, the project emphasizes providing users with customizable summarization options, enhancing usability across diverse domains.

Detailed Plan:

1. Text Preprocessing:

- Use natural language processing (NLP) libraries like NLTK or spaCy to preprocess the text.
- Tasks include:
    - Tokenizing sentences and words.
    - Removing stopwords, punctuation, and irrelevant characters.
    - Converting all text to lowercase for consistency.
    - Lemmatization or stemming to standardize word forms.
- Handle special cases like numerical data, dates, and named entities to preserve essential information.

- Validate the preprocessing pipeline to ensure no loss of critical data.

2. Extractive Summarization:

- Implement extractive techniques that identify the most significant sentences from the text.
- Use algorithms such as:
  - **TextRank:** A graph-based algorithm that ranks sentences based on their importance and interconnectivity.
  - **TF-IDF (Term Frequency-Inverse Document Frequency):** Scores sentences based on the uniqueness and relevance of their words.
- Combine heuristics like sentence position, keyword density, and topic coverage for better results.
- Visualize sentence importance scores to assist in fine-tuning the extractive process.

3. Abstractive Summarization:

- Employ transformer-based models for generating summaries that paraphrase and restructure content:
  - Use models like **BART** (Bidirectional and Auto-Regressive Transformers) or **GPT** (Generative Pre-trained Transformer).
  - Fine-tune these models on summarization datasets like CNN/Daily Mail or Gigaword to adapt them to specific use cases.
  - Balance between conciseness and informativeness by adjusting model parameters like length penalties.

- Incorporate reinforcement learning techniques for improved abstractive summaries.

4. Performance Evaluation:

    - Measure the quality of summaries using evaluation metrics such as:
        - **ROUGE (Recall-Oriented Understudy for Gisting Evaluation):** Compares overlaps between generated summaries and reference summaries.
        - **BLEU (Bilingual Evaluation Understudy):** Assesses the quality of generated text by comparing it to human-written text.
    - Conduct user surveys to gather qualitative feedback on clarity, accuracy, and relevance.
    - Perform A/B testing to identify the most user-preferred summarization models.

5. Deployment:

    - Develop a user-friendly web application with:
        - Options to upload text files, paste content, or input URLs for summarization.
        - Real-time feedback and results display.
    - Use frameworks like Flask or FastAPI for backend services and React or Vue.js for front-end development.
    - Integrate cloud services like AWS or Azure for scalability and faster inference times.
    - Include user authentication features for saving summaries or processing confidential documents.

6. Advanced Features:

- Enable language detection and support multilingual summarization.
- Provide summarization options like "brief" or "detailed" based on user preferences.
- Include keyword extraction and topic modeling as supplementary features.
- Allow users to highlight specific sections for prioritization during summarization.
- Offer downloadable summary reports in formats like PDF or Word.

7. Scalability and Optimization:

- Use GPU acceleration and model quantization techniques to optimize performance.
- Employ distributed computing for handling large-scale summarization tasks.
- Implement caching mechanisms for frequently requested documents or articles.
- Ensure compliance with data privacy laws like GDPR when handling sensitive content.

Outcome:

By implementing this project, users can quickly grasp the essence of lengthy texts without spending hours reading. The tool has applications in journalism, education, research, and business, making it a valuable asset for summarizing reports, articles, or meeting notes. Its advanced features and real-time deployment make it suitable for both individual and enterprise-level use cases.

Example Code:

```python
import nltk
from nltk.tokenize import sent_tokenize
from sklearn.feature_extraction.text import TfidfVectorizer
from sklearn.metrics.pairwise import cosine_similarity
import numpy as np

# Step 1: Preprocess Text
def preprocess_text(text):
    sentences = sent_tokenize(text)
    return sentences

# Step 2: Calculate Sentence Scores
def calculate_tfidf(sentences):
    vectorizer = TfidfVectorizer(stop_words='english')
    tfidf_matrix = vectorizer.fit_transform(sentences)
    scores = cosine_similarity(tfidf_matrix, tfidf_matrix)
    return scores

# Step 3: Rank Sentences
def rank_sentences(scores, sentences):
    ranked = np.argsort(np.sum(scores, axis=1))[-5:][::-1]  # Top 5 sentences
    summary = [sentences[i] for i in ranked]
    return " ".join(summary)

# Example Usage
if __name__ == "__main__":
    text = """
    Artificial intelligence and machine learning are transforming industries worldwide. They enable businesses to make data-driven decisions and automate processes. These technologies are also advancing fields like healthcare, education, and transportation. However, challenges such as ethical concerns, bias, and data privacy remain crucial areas of focus.
```

```
"""

sentences = preprocess_text(text)
scores = calculate_tfidf(sentences)
summary = rank_sentences(scores, sentences)
print("Summary:")
print(summary)
```

Project 6: Recommendation System for E-Commerce

Objective:

To develop a recommendation engine that suggests products based on user behavior, improving user experience and increasing sales conversions. The system will leverage collaborative and content-based filtering, enhanced by advanced machine learning techniques for personalized recommendations.

Detailed Plan:
1. Data Collection:

- Gather user and product data from e-commerce platforms, including:
    - Purchase history, clickstream data, and product ratings.
    - Product attributes such as categories, price, and brand.
- Use APIs or web scraping tools like BeautifulSoup for data extraction.

- Ensure data privacy and comply with regulations like GDPR.

2. Data Preprocessing:

- Clean and preprocess the data by:
    - Handling missing values and outliers.
    - Normalizing numerical features like price and ratings.
    - Encoding categorical data such as product categories and user demographics.
- Create user-product interaction matrices for collaborative filtering.

3. Model Building:

- Implement recommendation techniques:
    - **Collaborative Filtering:**
        - User-based filtering: Recommends products based on similar users' preferences.
        - Item-based filtering: Suggests items similar to those a user has interacted with.
    - **Content-Based Filtering:**
        - Uses product features and user preferences for recommendations.
- Use advanced techniques like:
    - **Matrix Factorization:** Apply Singular Value Decomposition (SVD) or Alternating Least Squares (ALS) to discover latent features.
    - **Deep Learning:**

- Employ neural collaborative filtering or autoencoders for enhanced predictions.
- Use models like Wide & Deep or embeddings from transformer architectures for scalability.

4. Performance Evaluation:

- Split data into training and test sets for validation.
- Use evaluation metrics such as:
  - Root Mean Squared Error (RMSE) and Mean Absolute Error (MAE) for rating predictions.
  - Precision, Recall, and F1-score for ranking accuracy.
  - Hit Rate or Coverage to evaluate the diversity of recommendations.

5. Deployment:

- Develop an API using frameworks like Flask or FastAPI to serve recommendations.
- Integrate the API with the e-commerce platform's front-end for real-time user interactions.
- Deploy the model on cloud platforms like AWS or Google Cloud for scalability and performance.

6. Advanced Features:

- Personalize recommendations based on contextual information such as time, location, and device.
- Implement a hybrid system combining collaborative and content-based filtering for improved accuracy.

- Add a feedback loop to learn from user interactions and improve suggestions.
- Include explainability features to show users why certain products are recommended.

7. Optimization and Scalability:

- Use parallel computing and GPU acceleration for faster model training.
- Optimize memory usage for handling large-scale datasets.
- Employ caching mechanisms to store frequently accessed recommendations.

Outcome:

The recommendation system will enhance user engagement by providing personalized product suggestions, leading to increased sales and improved customer satisfaction. It will also demonstrate the power of data-driven decision-making in the e-commerce industry.

Example Code:

```
import pandas as pd
from surprise import Dataset, Reader, SVD
from surprise.model_selection import train_test_split, accuracy

# Step 1: Load Data
data = {
   'user_id': [1, 1, 2, 2, 3, 3],
   'item_id': [101, 102, 101, 103, 102, 104],
   'rating': [5, 3, 4, 2, 1, 5]
}
df = pd.DataFrame(data)
```

```python
reader = Reader(rating_scale=(1, 5))
data = Dataset.load_from_df(df[['user_id', 'item_id', 'rating']], reader)

# Step 2: Train-Test Split
trainset, testset = train_test_split(data, test_size=0.2)

# Step 3: Train Model
model = SVD()
model.fit(trainset)

# Step 4: Evaluate Model
predictions = model.test(testset)
accuracy.rmse(predictions)

# Step 5: Make Recommendations
def recommend(user_id, model, data, n=5):
    all_items = set(df['item_id'].unique())
    rated_items = set(df[df['user_id'] == user_id]['item_id'])
    unrated_items = all_items - rated_items

    recommendations = [
        (item, model.predict(user_id, item).est)
        for item in unrated_items
    ]
    recommendations.sort(key=lambda x: x[1], reverse=True)
    return recommendations[:n]

# Example Usage
print(recommend(1, model, data))
```

Project 7: Time Series Forecasting for Sales Data

Objective:

To develop a time series forecasting model that predicts future sales, aiding inventory management and revenue planning. This project helps businesses make informed, data-driven decisions to optimize resources and meet demand effectively.

Detailed Plan:

1. Data Collection:

- Gather historical sales data from sources such as:
    - Point-of-Sale (POS) systems in physical stores.
    - Transaction logs from online stores.
    - Data from external sources like holiday calendars or weather APIs.
- Include fields like timestamps, product categories, locations, and sales volumes for comprehensive analysis.

2. Exploratory Data Analysis (EDA):

- Visualize sales trends over time to identify:
    - Seasonal patterns (e.g., holidays, weekends).
    - Long-term trends (growth or decline in sales).
    - Irregularities or outliers (sudden spikes or drops).
- Use techniques such as:
    - Decomposition of time series data into trend, seasonal, and residual components.

- Correlation analysis to understand relationships between variables like price and sales.

3. Data Preprocessing:

- Handle missing values using interpolation or forward/backward filling methods.
- Normalize or standardize numerical features to ensure consistency.
- Encode categorical variables like product categories or regions if needed.
- Aggregate data to appropriate granularity (daily, weekly, or monthly) based on business requirements.

4. Model Selection and Training:

- Train forecasting models based on the nature of the sales data:
    - **ARIMA (AutoRegressive Integrated Moving Average):** Suitable for non-seasonal time series data.
    - **SARIMA (Seasonal ARIMA):** Handles seasonal variations in sales.
    - **Prophet (by Facebook):** Robust for time series with missing data or strong seasonality.
    - **LSTM (Long Short-Term Memory networks):** For capturing non-linear patterns and long-term dependencies.
- Split data into training and test sets, reserving the most recent data for validation.

- Tune hyperparameters using grid search or automated tools like Optuna.

5. Model Evaluation:

- Use metrics like:
    - Mean Absolute Error (MAE)
    - Mean Squared Error (MSE)
    - Mean Absolute Percentage Error (MAPE)
- Perform backtesting to evaluate model predictions against historical data.
- Compare models to select the one with the best trade-off between accuracy and complexity.

6. Deployment and Visualization:

- Develop interactive dashboards using tools like Tableau, Power BI, or Dash.
    - Display metrics such as predicted sales, confidence intervals, and trends.
    - Allow filtering by time period, product category, or location.
- Integrate the model into inventory or ERP systems for real-time decision-making.

7. Scalability and Optimization:

- Use cloud platforms like AWS or Google Cloud for handling large datasets and deploying models at scale.
- Optimize forecasting pipelines for real-time predictions.

- Implement scheduled retraining with updated data to maintain accuracy.

Outcome:

The forecasting model provides actionable insights into future sales, enabling businesses to optimize inventory levels, plan revenue strategies, and respond proactively to market demands. It empowers data-driven decision-making to enhance operational efficiency and profitability.

Example Code:

```
import pandas as pd
from statsmodels.tsa.statespace.sarimax import SARIMAX
from sklearn.metrics import mean_absolute_error, mean_squared_error
import matplotlib.pyplot as plt

# Step 1: Load Data
data = pd.read_csv('sales_data.csv', parse_dates=['date'], index_col='date')

# Step 2: Visualize Data
data['sales'].plot(title='Sales Over Time', figsize=(10, 6))
plt.show()

# Step 3: Train-Test Split
train = data[:'2022-12-31']
test = data['2023-01-01':]

# Step 4: Train SARIMA Model
model = SARIMAX(train['sales'], order=(1, 1, 1), seasonal_order=(1, 1, 1, 12))
results = model.fit()

# Step 5: Forecast
forecast = results.get_forecast(steps=len(test))
```

```
forecast_index = test.index
forecast_values = forecast.predicted_mean
confidence_intervals = forecast.conf_int()

# Step 6: Evaluate
mae = mean_absolute_error(test['sales'], forecast_values)
mse = mean_squared_error(test['sales'], forecast_values)
print(f"MAE: {mae}, MSE: {mse}")

# Step 7: Visualize Predictions
plt.figure(figsize=(10, 6))
plt.plot(train['sales'], label='Training Data')
plt.plot(test['sales'], label='Actual Sales', color='orange')
plt.plot(forecast_index, forecast_values, label='Forecast', color='green')
plt.fill_between(forecast_index, confidence_intervals.iloc[:, 0],
confidence_intervals.iloc[:, 1], color='green', alpha=0.2)
plt.legend()
plt.title('Sales Forecasting')
plt.show()
```

Project 8: Object Detection in Images

Objective:

To identify and locate objects within images, supporting applications that require detailed object localization, such as autonomous vehicles, security systems, and retail analytics.

Detailed Plan:
1. Dataset Selection:

- Use publicly available datasets like:

- - **COCO (Common Objects in Context):** Contains labeled images with bounding boxes for various objects.
  - **Pascal VOC (Visual Object Classes):** Provides annotations for 20 object categories.
- Optionally, collect domain-specific data and annotate using tools like LabelImg for custom applications.

2. Data Preprocessing:

- Resize images to a consistent dimension (e.g., 416x416 for YOLO).
- Normalize pixel values to a range of [0, 1] or [-1, 1].
- Augment data with transformations like rotation, flipping, and scaling to enhance model robustness.
- Split the dataset into training, validation, and test sets.

3. Model Selection and Training:

- Choose object detection algorithms based on requirements:
  - **YOLO (You Only Look Once):** Fast and suitable for real-time applications.
  - **Faster R-CNN (Region-Based Convolutional Neural Networks):** High accuracy but computationally intensive.
  - **SSD (Single Shot MultiBox Detector):** Balances speed and accuracy.
- Train models using deep learning frameworks like TensorFlow or PyTorch:
  - Initialize with pre-trained weights from ImageNet or COCO for transfer learning.

- Fine-tune hyperparameters like learning rate, batch size, and confidence thresholds.

4. Performance Evaluation:

- Use metrics such as:
    - **mAP (Mean Average Precision):** Measures detection accuracy across all classes.
    - **IoU (Intersection over Union):** Evaluates the overlap between predicted and actual bounding boxes.
- Analyze confusion matrices to identify and address misclassifications.

5. Optimization for Real-Time Detection:

- Optimize models for edge devices (e.g., drones, mobile phones):
    - Quantize models to reduce size and inference time.
    - Use TensorRT or OpenVINO for hardware acceleration.
- Implement non-max suppression (NMS) to remove redundant bounding boxes.

6. Deployment:

- Deploy object detection models as APIs or standalone applications:
    - Use Flask or FastAPI for REST API development.

- - Integrate with IoT devices for real-time video feed analysis.
  - Test models in real-world scenarios to ensure robustness.

7. Scalability and Maintenance:

- Regularly retrain models with updated data to improve performance.
- Implement logging and monitoring tools for deployment environments.
- Scale deployments using cloud services like AWS, Google Cloud, or Azure.

Outcome:

The object detection system will accurately identify and locate objects in images, enabling applications in autonomous navigation, surveillance, and automated checkout systems. The solution combines accuracy with real-time efficiency for practical use cases.

Example Code:
```
import cv2
import numpy as np
import tensorflow as tf

# Step 1: Load Pre-Trained YOLO Model
yolo_net = cv2.dnn.readNet('yolov4.weights', 'yolov4.cfg')
layers = yolo_net.getLayerNames()
out_layers = [layers[i - 1] for i in yolo_net.getUnconnectedOutLayers()]

# Step 2: Load COCO Classes
with open('coco.names', 'r') as f:
```

```python
    classes = f.read().strip().split('\n')

# Step 3: Process Image
def detect_objects(image_path):
    image = cv2.imread(image_path)
    height, width = image.shape[:2]

    # Preprocess Input
    blob = cv2.dnn.blobFromImage(image, 1/255.0, (416, 416), swapRB=True, crop=False)
    yolo_net.setInput(blob)

    # Run Detection
    outputs = yolo_net.forward(out_layers)
    boxes, confidences, class_ids = [], [], []

    for output in outputs:
        for detection in output:
            scores = detection[5:]
            class_id = np.argmax(scores)
            confidence = scores[class_id]

            if confidence > 0.5:
                box = detection[:4] * np.array([width, height, width, height])
                (center_x, center_y, box_w, box_h) = box.astype('int')

                x = int(center_x - (box_w / 2))
                y = int(center_y - (box_h / 2))
                boxes.append([x, y, int(box_w), int(box_h)])
                confidences.append(float(confidence))
                class_ids.append(class_id)

    # Apply Non-Max Suppression
    indices = cv2.dnn.NMSBoxes(boxes, confidences, 0.5, 0.4)
    for i in indices.flatten():
        x, y, w, h = boxes[i]
        label = str(classes[class_ids[i]])
        confidence = confidences[i]
```

```
    cv2.rectangle(image, (x, y), (x + w, y + h), (0, 255, 0), 2)
    cv2.putText(image, f"{label}: {confidence:.2f}", (x, y - 10),
cv2.FONT_HERSHEY_SIMPLEX, 0.5, (0, 255, 0), 2)

    cv2.imshow('Detection', image)
    cv2.waitKey(0)
    cv2.destroyAllWindows()

# Example Usage
detect_objects('example_image.jpg')
```

Project 9: Fraud Detection in Financial Transactions

Objective:

To detect fraudulent transactions using anomaly detection techniques, reducing financial losses and enhancing customer trust. This system will identify suspicious activities in real-time to enable quick action and prevent fraud.

Detailed Plan:
1. Data Collection:

- Gather transactional data, including:
    - Timestamps
    - Transaction amounts
    - User IDs and account details
    - Transaction types (e.g., online, in-store)
    - Geolocation and device information
- Source data from financial institutions, payment gateways, or simulated datasets.

- Ensure data privacy and compliance with regulations like GDPR.

2. Data Preprocessing:

- Handle missing or incomplete data using imputation techniques.
- Normalize numerical features, such as transaction amounts, for uniformity.
- Encode categorical features like transaction types and user demographics.
- Detect and handle data imbalances:
    - Use oversampling techniques like SMOTE (Synthetic Minority Oversampling Technique).
    - Undersample majority classes if necessary.
- Identify and remove outliers using statistical methods or clustering algorithms.

3. Model Selection and Training:

- Explore machine learning models for fraud detection:
    - **Supervised Learning Models:**
        - Random Forest
        - XGBoost
    - **Unsupervised Learning Models:**
        - Isolation Forest
        - K-Means Clustering for anomaly detection
    - **Deep Learning Models:**
        - Autoencoders for unsupervised anomaly detection
        - LSTMs for sequential data analysis

- Use feature engineering to create meaningful predictors, such as:
    - Average transaction value per user
    - Frequency of transactions
    - Time between successive transactions
- Split the dataset into training, validation, and test sets.

4. Performance Evaluation:

- Evaluate models using metrics specific to fraud detection:
    - Precision, Recall, and F1-score to handle class imbalance.
    - Area Under the ROC Curve (AUC-ROC) for overall model performance.
- Perform cross-validation to ensure robustness and avoid overfitting.

5. Real-Time Fraud Detection System:

- Implement the trained model as a service:
    - Use Flask or FastAPI to create a REST API for model predictions.
    - Process transactions in real-time to flag suspicious activities.
- Integrate the system with alert mechanisms:
    - Send email or SMS notifications to users and administrators.
    - Implement a dashboard to review flagged transactions.

6. Scalability and Maintenance:

- Deploy the system on scalable platforms like AWS or Google Cloud.
- Use load balancers and distributed processing to handle high transaction volumes.
- Continuously retrain the model with new data to adapt to evolving fraud patterns.
- Monitor system performance and add features based on user feedback.

Outcome:

The fraud detection system will effectively identify potentially fraudulent transactions, enabling financial institutions to mitigate risks and enhance security. Real-time capabilities ensure swift responses, reducing financial losses and improving user confidence.

Example Code:

```
import pandas as pd
import numpy as np
from sklearn.ensemble import IsolationForest
from sklearn.model_selection import train_test_split
from sklearn.metrics import classification_report, roc_auc_score

# Step 1: Load Data
data = pd.read_csv('transactions.csv')

# Step 2: Preprocess Data
data['amount_normalized'] = (data['amount'] - data['amount'].mean()) / data['amount'].std()
data = pd.get_dummies(data, columns=['transaction_type'], drop_first=True)
```

```python
# Step 3: Train-Test Split
X = data.drop(['is_fraud'], axis=1)
y = data['is_fraud']
X_train, X_test, y_train, y_test = train_test_split(X, y, test_size=0.3, random_state=42)

# Step 4: Train Isolation Forest
model = IsolationForest(contamination=0.01, random_state=42)
model.fit(X_train)

# Step 5: Predict and Evaluate
predictions = model.predict(X_test)
predictions = [1 if p == -1 else 0 for p in predictions]
print(classification_report(y_test, predictions))
auc = roc_auc_score(y_test, predictions)
print(f"AUC-ROC Score: {auc}")

# Step 6: Real-Time Prediction Example
def predict_transaction(transaction):
    transaction_df = pd.DataFrame([transaction])
    transaction_df['amount_normalized'] = (transaction_df['amount'] - data['amount'].mean()) / data['amount'].std()
    transaction_df = pd.get_dummies(transaction_df, columns=['transaction_type'], drop_first=True)
    prediction = model.predict(transaction_df)
    return "Fraud" if prediction[0] == -1 else "Legitimate"

# Example Usage
new_transaction = {
    'amount': 1200,
    'transaction_type': 'online',
    'user_age': 35,
    'device': 'mobile'
}
print(predict_transaction(new_transaction))
```

Project 10: Chatbot for Customer Support

Objective:

To create an intelligent chatbot capable of handling customer queries efficiently, reducing response times and streamlining customer support operations. The chatbot will leverage advanced Natural Language Processing (NLP) techniques to understand and respond to user intents effectively.

Detailed Plan:
1. Dataset Selection and Preparation:

- Use publicly available datasets like:
    - **Cornell Movie Dialogues Dataset:** Contains conversational exchanges useful for training dialogue systems.
    - **Customer Support Datasets:** For domain-specific training, gather chat transcripts or FAQs from customer support teams.
- Preprocess the data by:
    - Removing special characters and irrelevant tokens.
    - Normalizing text by converting to lowercase and stemming/lemmatizing words.
    - Annotating datasets with intents and entities for supervised training.

2. Natural Language Understanding (NLU):

- Implement NLU using frameworks such as:

- **Rasa:** An open-source platform for building conversational AI with support for intent classification and entity recognition.
- **Dialogflow:** Google's cloud-based NLU tool for easy integration with various platforms.
- Train the chatbot to recognize intents like:
  - FAQ queries (e.g., "What is your return policy?")
  - Transactional queries (e.g., "Track my order.")
  - Small talk (e.g., "How are you?")
- Extract entities (e.g., order ID, dates, product names) from user input for contextual responses.

3. Dialog Management:

- Use a rule-based or machine learning-based approach to manage conversations:
  - Define conversation flows and fallback actions for unrecognized intents.
  - Implement context handling to maintain state across multi-turn dialogues.
  - Use pre-built modules in Rasa or Dialogflow for slot filling and intent chaining.

4. Model Deployment and Integration:

- Integrate the chatbot with messaging platforms such as:
  - WhatsApp, Facebook Messenger, Slack, or a custom web-based chat interface.
- Deploy the chatbot using:
  - **Flask/Django:** For API development.

- o **AWS Lambda or Google Cloud Functions:** For scalable serverless deployment.
- Enable real-time analytics to track user interactions and performance metrics.

5. Improvement and Feedback Loop:

- Gather user feedback by monitoring chat logs and user ratings for responses.
- Continuously improve the chatbot by:
    - o Adding new intents and training examples.
    - o Enhancing response quality with pre-trained language models like GPT-3 or BERT.
    - o Conducting A/B testing to evaluate changes.

6. Advanced Features:

- Enable voice support using Speech-to-Text (STT) and Text-to-Speech (TTS) integrations.
- Personalize interactions based on user history and preferences.
- Integrate with backend systems (e.g., CRM, order tracking) for dynamic responses.

Outcome:

The chatbot will effectively handle customer inquiries, reducing the workload on human agents and improving response times. This intelligent system will enhance customer satisfaction and operational efficiency, with the ability to scale as the business grows.

Example Code:

```python
from rasa_sdk import Action, Tracker
from rasa_sdk.executor import CollectingDispatcher

class ActionTrackOrder(Action):

    def name(self):
        return "action_track_order"

    def run(self, dispatcher: CollectingDispatcher,
            tracker: Tracker,
            domain: dict):

        order_id = tracker.get_slot('order_id')
        if order_id:
            # Simulate order tracking logic
            response = f"Your order with ID {order_id} is on the way!"
        else:
            response = "I couldn't find your order ID. Can you please provide it?"

        dispatcher.utter_message(text=response)
        return []

# Example NLU Configuration
nlu_data = {
    "intents": [
        {
            "intent": "track_order",
            "examples": [
                "Track my order",
                "Where is my package?",
                "I want to track order ID 12345"
            ]
        }
    ]
}
```

```
# Example Training Command
# rasa train

# Deployment Command
# rasa run --enable-api
```

By implementing these projects, developers can gain hands-on experience in Python-based AI development, learn best practices, and solve real-world problems effectively. Each project demonstrates the versatility and potential of AI across various domains, equipping practitioners with the tools to excel in the field.

12. Resources for Learning Python-Based AI and ML

Python has emerged as one of the most powerful and versatile programming languages for Artificial Intelligence (AI) and Machine Learning (ML). With an extensive ecosystem of libraries, tools, and community resources, Python enables developers to create sophisticated models with relative ease. This section will provide a comprehensive guide to the top Python libraries, recommended learning resources, and strategies for staying updated with the latest AI and ML trends.

Top Python Libraries for AI and ML

Python's dominance in AI and ML is largely due to its robust library ecosystem. Here are the top libraries you need to know:

1. **NumPy**:
    - Foundation for numerical computing in Python.
    - Provides powerful tools for working with arrays, matrices, and numerical data.
    - Essential for performing data preprocessing and mathematical operations in ML workflows.
2. **Pandas**:
    - Simplifies data manipulation and analysis.
    - Offers intuitive DataFrame structures for handling tabular data.
    - Frequently used for cleaning, exploring, and preparing data for ML models.

3. **Scikit-Learn**:
   - A cornerstone library for traditional machine learning.
   - Features algorithms for classification, regression, clustering, and dimensionality reduction.
   - Integrates tools for model evaluation, hyperparameter tuning, and pipeline construction.
4. **TensorFlow and PyTorch**:
   - TensorFlow:
     - Developed by Google, it is widely used for deep learning.
     - Supports distributed training and deployment across platforms.
     - Offers high-level APIs like Keras for building neural networks.
   - PyTorch:
     - Favored by researchers for its dynamic computation graph.
     - Easier debugging and greater flexibility in experimentation.
     - Excellent for prototyping and scaling deep learning models.
5. **Keras**:
   - High-level API built on top of TensorFlow.
   - Simplifies the process of creating, training, and deploying neural networks.
   - Ideal for beginners due to its user-friendly syntax.
6. **Matplotlib and Seaborn**:

- Visualization libraries for creating insightful charts and plots.
- Help in understanding data distributions, trends, and model performance.

7. **NLTK and SpaCy**:
    - Focused on natural language processing (NLP).
    - NLTK:
        - Comprehensive set of tools for text processing, tokenization, and stemming.
    - SpaCy:
        - Optimized for large-scale NLP tasks.
        - Features pre-trained models for part-of-speech tagging, dependency parsing, and entity recognition.

8. **OpenCV**:
    - A library for computer vision tasks.
    - Useful for image preprocessing, feature detection, and object recognition.

9. **Hugging Face Transformers**:
    - State-of-the-art library for NLP tasks.
    - Supports models like BERT, GPT, and RoBERTa.
    - Simplifies fine-tuning pre-trained transformers for custom applications.

10. **XGBoost and LightGBM**:
    - Specialized libraries for gradient boosting algorithms.
    - Commonly used in data science competitions for their performance and efficiency.

Recommended Courses and My Books, Apps

To master Python-based AI and ML, the following courses, books, and apps are highly recommended:

1. **Apps:**
   - Python Programs
   - Learn Python
2. **Online Courses:**
   - Python Power Practice: 500+ Advanced Coding Challenges
   - 600+ Python Interview Questions - Practice Tests
3. **My Books:**
   - AI and ML for Developers: A Hands-On Guide
   - Learn Generative AI with PyTorch: Generative AI with PyTorch - Build GANs, VAEs, and More
   - Master Python in 7 Days: A Beginner's Guide to Programming Success
   - Python Mastery: 100 Essential Topics for Every Developer
   - Data Analytics for Dummies: Step-by-Step with Python

Staying Up-to-Date with AI Trends in Python

The field of AI and ML evolves rapidly, making it crucial to stay informed about the latest advancements and best practices. Here's how to keep up:

1. **Follow Influential Blogs and Websites:**
   - Towards Data Science (Medium)

- Analytics Vidhya
- KDnuggets
- TensorFlow and PyTorch official blogs
2. **Subscribe to Newsletters:**
   - The Batch by Andrew Ng
   - Import AI
   - AI Weekly
3. **Engage with Communities:**
   - Join forums like Reddit (r/MachineLearning, r/Python) and Stack Overflow.
   - Participate in meetups and webinars hosted by local AI/ML groups.
4. **Stay Active on GitHub:**
   - Follow repositories of popular libraries like Scikit-learn, TensorFlow, and Hugging Face.
   - Contribute to open-source projects to gain practical experience.
5. **Experiment with Emerging Tools:**
   - Explore cutting-edge frameworks like FastAI for rapid prototyping.
   - Try AutoML tools like H2O.ai or Google's AutoML for automated model building.

By leveraging these resources, aspiring AI and ML practitioners can develop a strong foundation, stay ahead of the curve, and contribute meaningfully to the rapidly growing field of artificial intelligence.

Made in the USA
Monee, IL
22 February 2025